The Raphael Cartoons

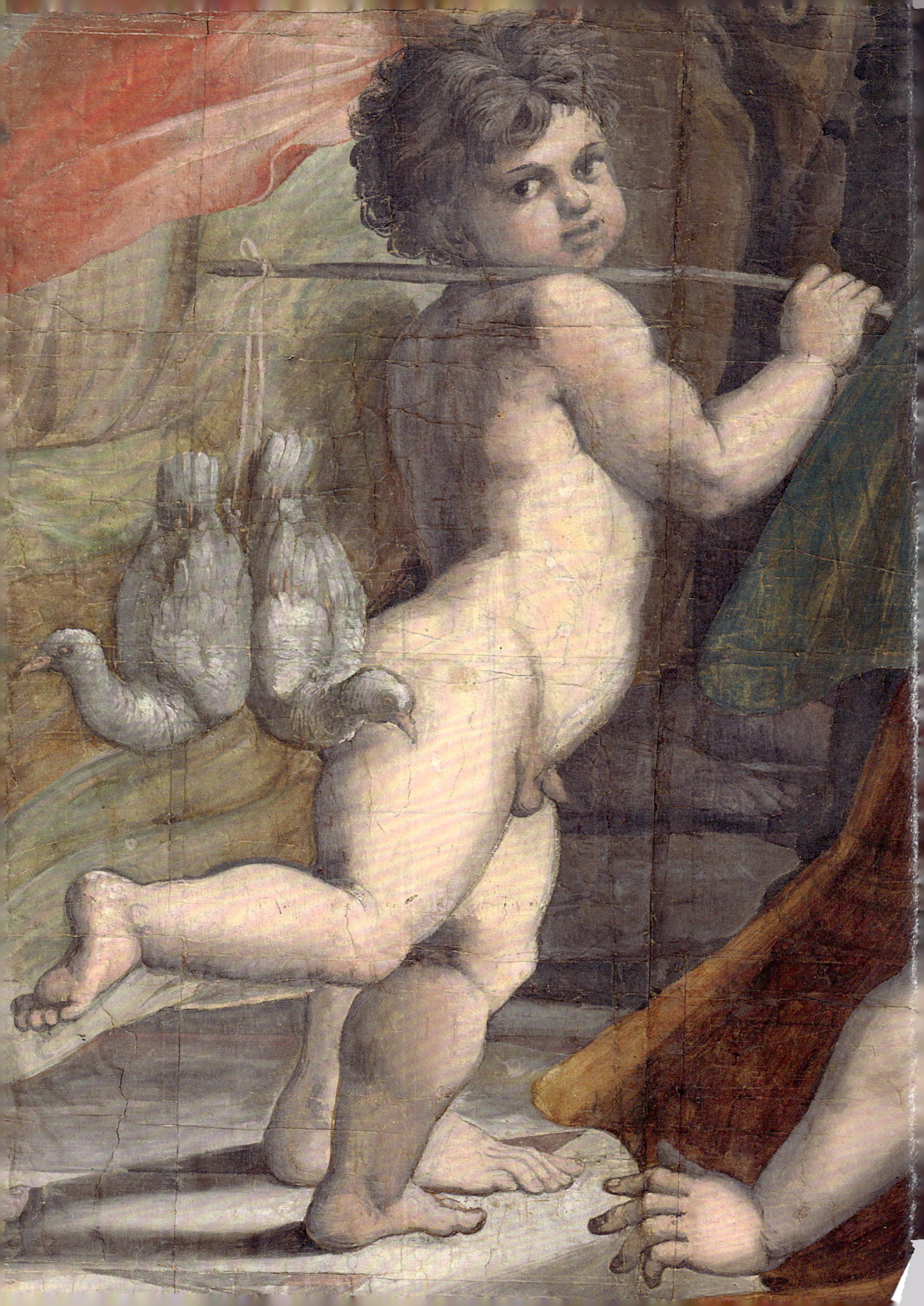

Edited by Ana Debenedetti

V&A Publishing

The Raphael Cartoons

First published by V&A Publishing, 2020
Victoria and Albert Museum
South Kensington
London SW7 2RL
vam.ac.uk/publishing

In collaboration with:

Photography of the Raphael
Cartoons supported by:

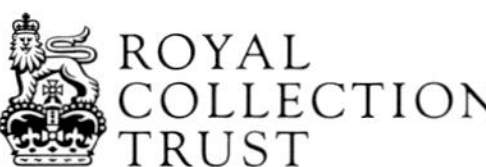

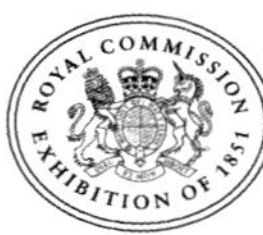

Distributed in North America by Abrams, an imprint of ABRAMS

ISBN 9781 83851 009 1

10 9 8 7 6 5 4 3 2
2024 2023 2022

A catalogue record for this book is available from the British Library.

Designer: Planning Unit
Origination: DL Imaging
New photography: Factum Foundation
Index: Hilary Bird
Printed in the UK

Front cover illustration: detail of *The Miraculous Draught of Fishes* (p. 19)

V&A Publishing

Supporting the world's leading
museum of art and design,
the Victoria and Albert
Museum, London

Contents

Director's Foreword   6
Tristram Hunt

The Museum Story:
An Introduction   10
Ana Debenedetti

The Raphael Cartoons   18

The Making of the Cartoons:
Raphael and his Workshop   26
Ana Debenedetti

Raphael's Tapestries
Past and Present   46
Alessandra Rodolfo

The Cartoons at
Hampton Court Palace   62
Brett Dolman

The Afterlife of the Cartoons:
Their Copies and British Art   76
Ana Debenedetti

Notes   95

Select Bibliography   103

Acknowledgements   109

Picture Credits   109

Index   110

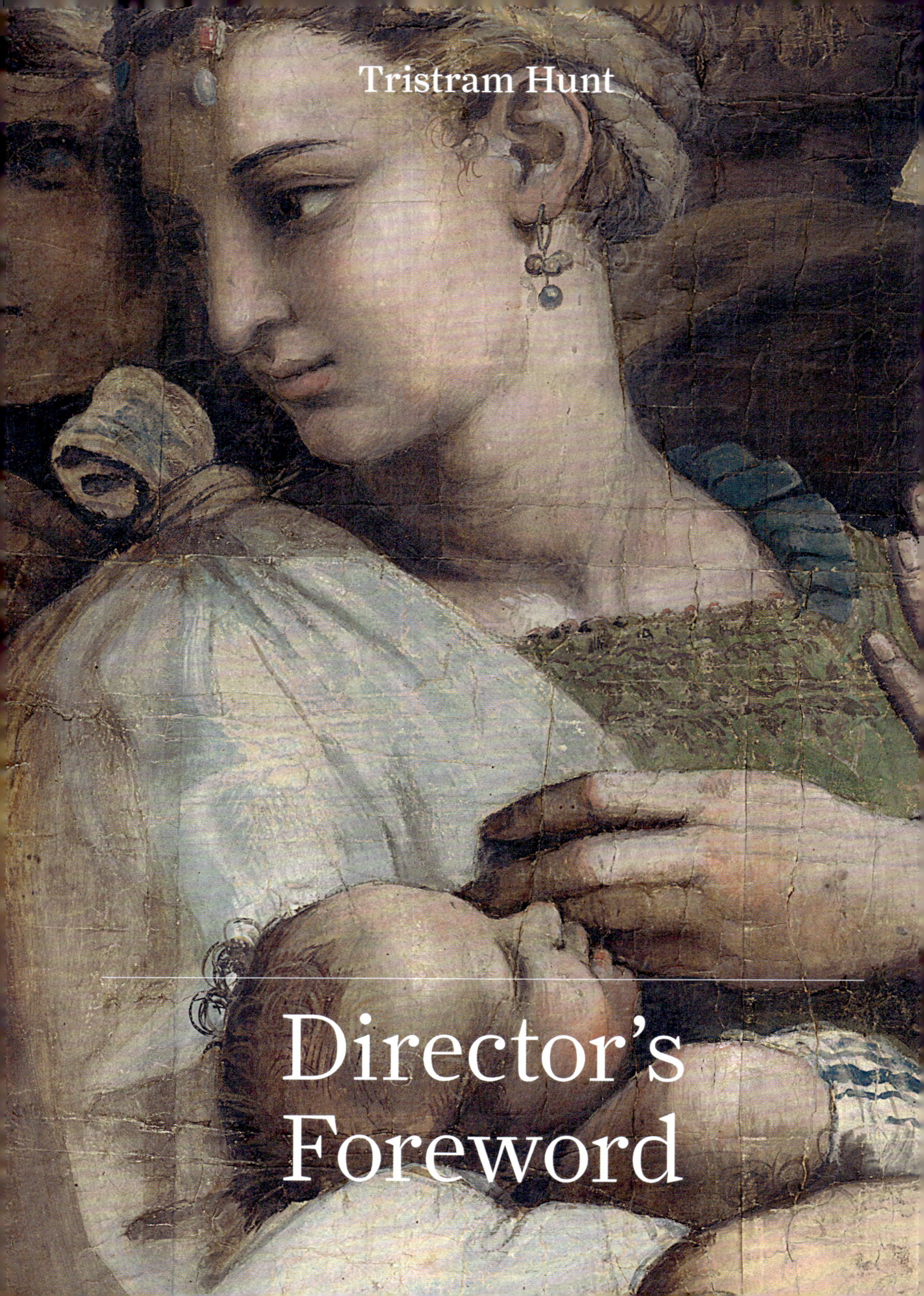

Tristram Hunt
Director's Foreword

For over 150 years, the Victoria and Albert Museum has had the privilege of hosting the seven surviving Raphael Cartoons: the only full-scale tapestry designs made by Raphael's hand. Their status as both working drawings and works of art in their own right, together with Prince Albert's deep admiration for Raphael's craftsmanship, led Queen Victoria to lend them to the museum. At the V&A, the Cartoons are still a personal loan by Her Majesty The Queen from the Royal Collection. They are widely celebrated as the greatest Renaissance treasures in the United Kingdom, the only monumental works by the master available outside Italy.

The Cartoons have gone through different phases of display and interpretation in the museum as scholarship moved on. Their relocation to the current gallery took place after the Second World War. Now commonly known as the Raphael Court, the gallery has the same dimensions as the Sistine Chapel in the Vatican, the original destination of the tapestries for which the Cartoons are the designs. For making the latest renovation possible, we are indebted to many generous donors, especially Lydia & Manfred Gorvy, Julia and Hans Rausing, American Express, Sir Michael and Lady Hintze, the Robert H. Smith Family Foundation and the American Friends of the V&A.

To mark the 500th anniversary of Raphael's death in 2020, the Royal Commission for the Exhibition of 1851's support has enabled us to undertake a major new study of these masterpieces. Cutting-edge technology provided by Adam Lowe and Factum Foundation has allowed curators and conservators to devise a new digital offer, making the detail of Raphael's beautiful images – once reserved for specialists only – available to the wider public. We can all now enjoy the extraordinarily preserved fresh colours of the Cartoons and gain further insight into Raphael's creative process and inventive genius.

This book expands on the findings made during past campaigns of photography and research. Rather than focusing on their making alone, it recontextualizes the role and complex history of the Cartoons over 500 years, from the prestigious commission made by Pope Leo X to their reception on the Continent, and remarkable legacy in Great Britain. Raphael's Cartoons have achieved a long-lasting artistic authority and we hope they will continue to inspire for generations to come.

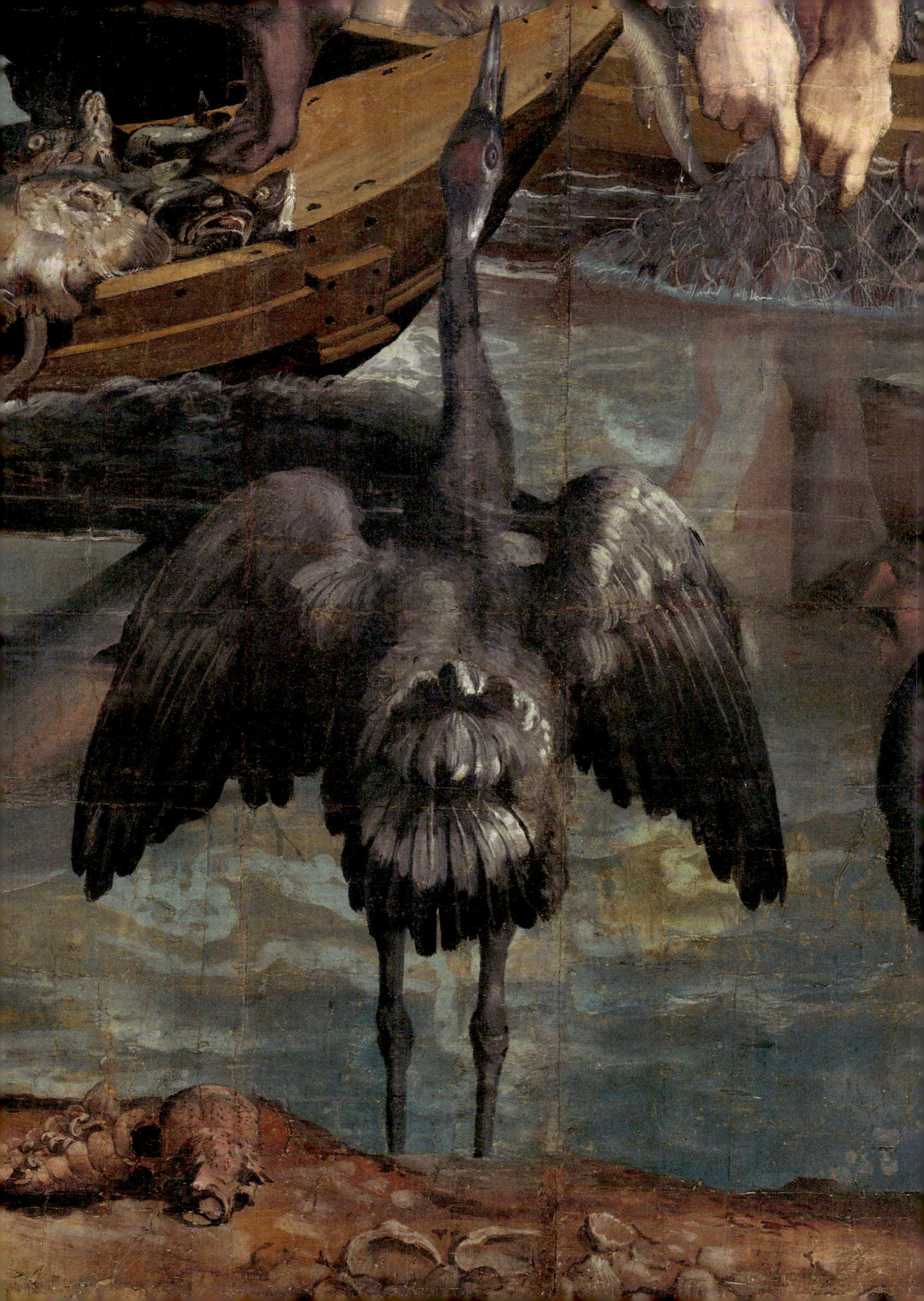

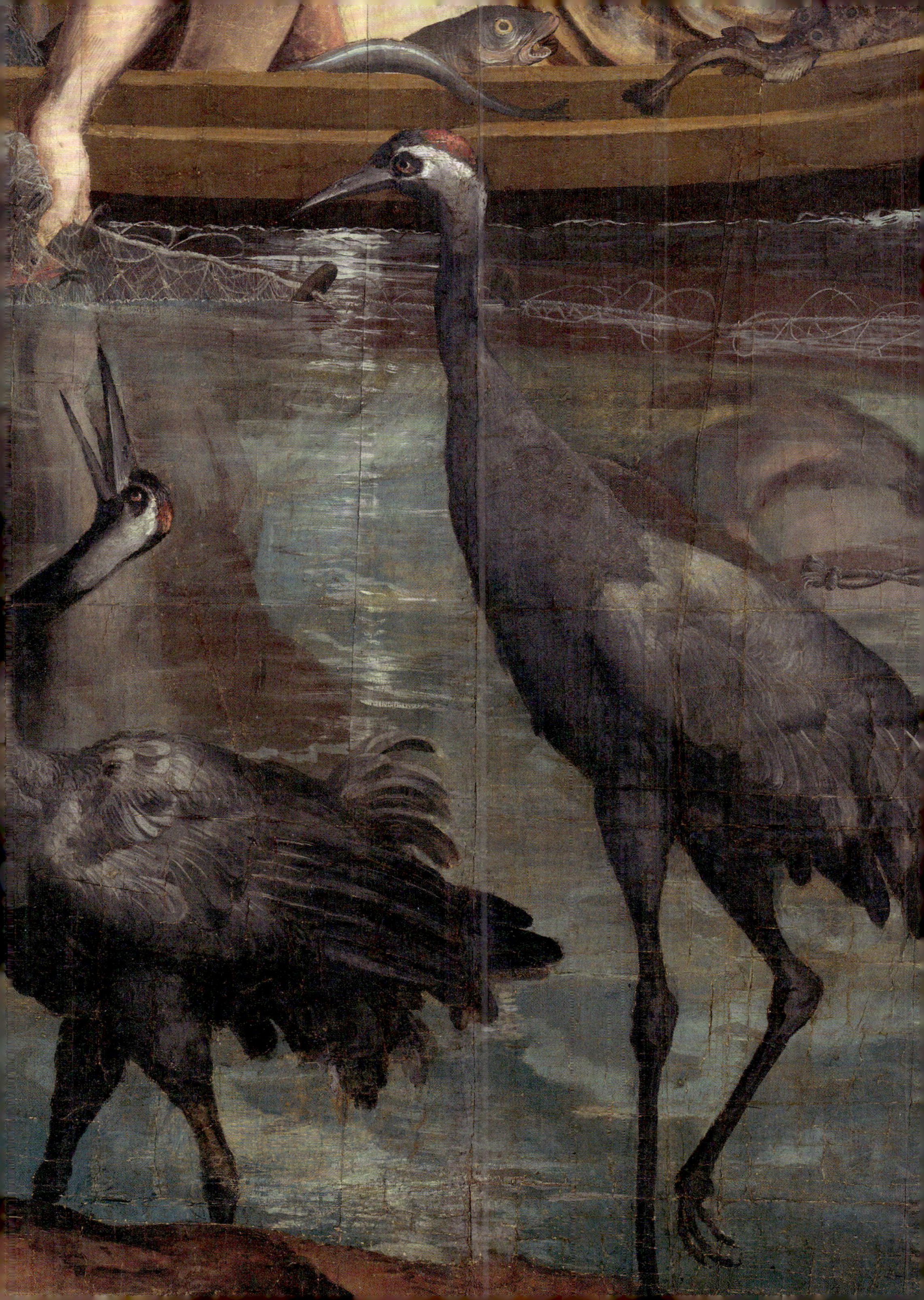

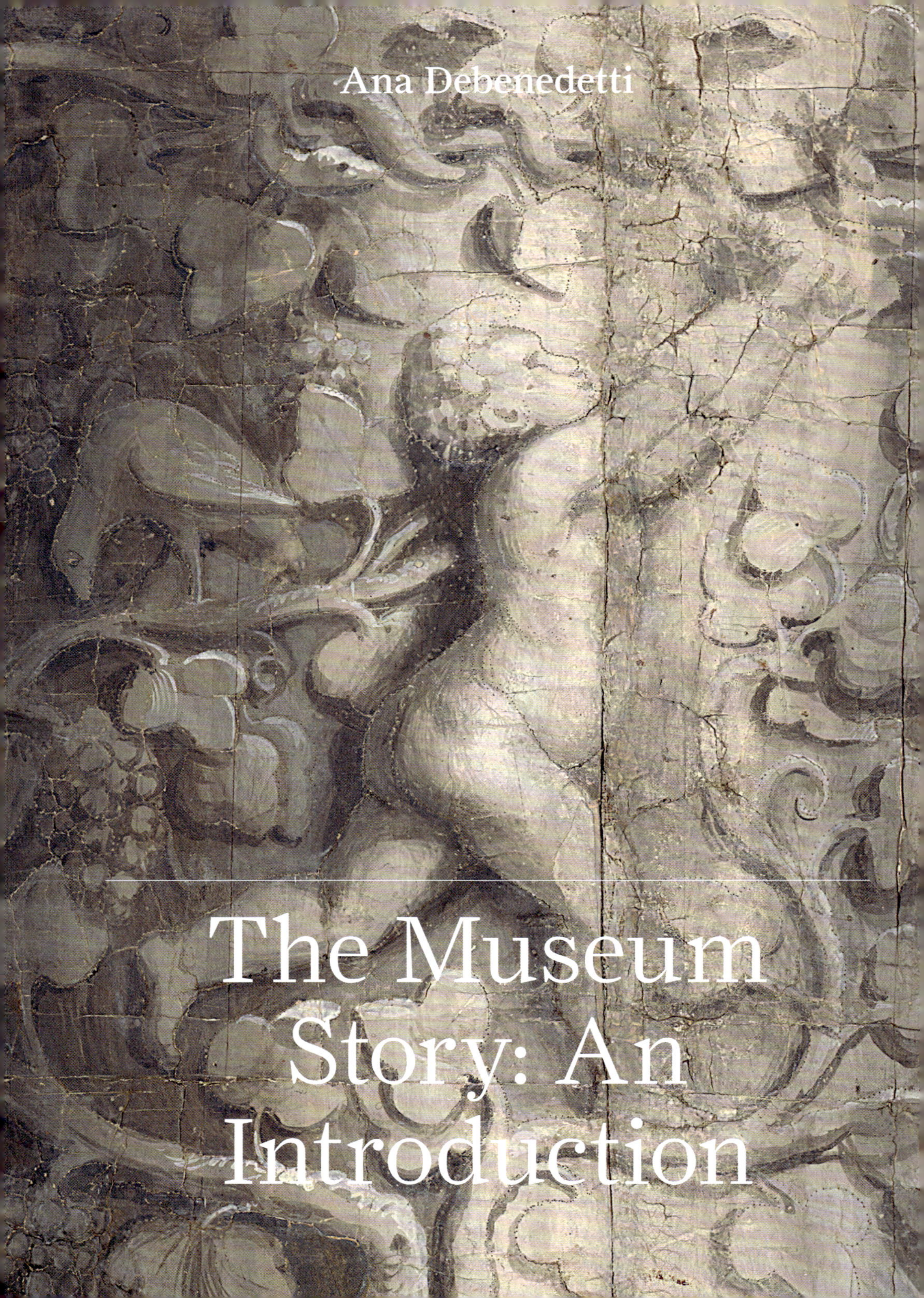

The Museum Story: An Introduction

The full-scale designs for tapestries, better known as the Raphael Cartoons, that everyone can enjoy today in Gallery 48A in the V&A, were commissioned by Pope Leo X for the Sistine Chapel in the Vatican Palace, Rome, sometime between March 1513 (the date of his election) and June 1515 (the date of the first known payment received by Raphael). Raphael was at the time the leading artist in the city and already engaged with the decoration of the Vatican Palace. After a convoluted history, during which the location of the Cartoons was unknown for a number of years, followed by their remarkable arrival in Britain in the early seventeenth century, their museum story effectively begins in 1865, 350 years after their creation. In April of that year the Cartoons, which had been on and off display at Hampton Court Palace since the reign of King William III (r.1689–1702), were transferred in large crates on horse-drawn carts to the South Kensington Museum, later renamed the Victoria and Albert Museum (1).

The Cartoons had become increasingly accessible with the accession of Queen Victoria in 1837 and the subsequent opening to the public of Hampton Court Palace. They entered a new phase of their history a few years later, thanks to an ambitious enterprise on the part of Albert, Prince Consort to the Queen (1819–1861). Known as the 'Raphael Collection', this was a pioneering contribution to the world of connoisseurship driven by an educational agenda. With over 5,400 photographs and engravings, the collection was intended to be a 'worthy representation of the greatest and noblest genius in the history of art' with a didactic purpose:

> It would place before the student not only the entire series of the artist's works and demonstrate the general developement [*sic*] of his genius, but it would also explain the individual history of each of his conceptions, and would show how the first hasty sketch had ripened into the fully matured and conscientiously studied master piece.[1]

Prince Albert chose Raphael because 'he had always entertained the strongest predilection [for this master], whose place at the head of the artists of all schools and all times few will dispute'.[2] Michelangelo and Leonardo da Vinci were to follow but the premature death of the

Prince in 1861 prevented the further development of this venture. Such a predilection for Raphael extended to the interiors of the Royal Mausoleum at Frogmore, Queen Victoria and Prince Albert's final resting place, where the polychromatic decoration was inspired by the Renaissance master.

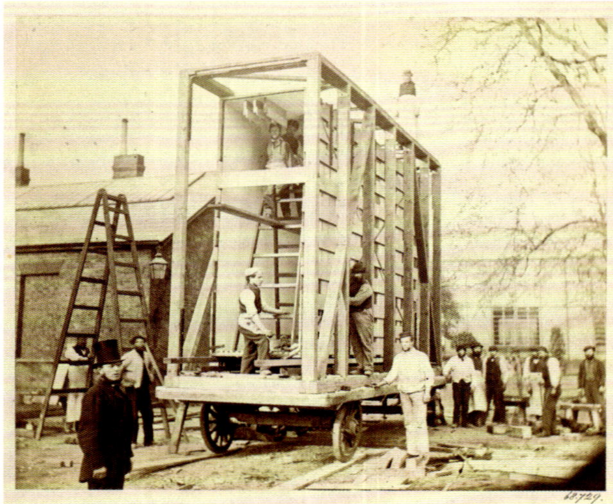

<< 1
Charles Thurston Thompson (1816–1868) and Benjamin L. Spackman (b.1834)
Transport of the Raphael Cartoons in large crates on horse-drawn carts from Hampton Court Palace to the South Kensington Museum, 1865

Albumen print
V&A: E.1090–1989

Prince Albert had taken a keen interest in the foundation of the South Kensington Museum, which followed a similar principle and originally grew out of the School of Design and the Museum of Manufactures. According to its first director Henry Cole (1808–1882), the museum's founding mission was to be 'a schoolroom for everyone'.[3] Prince Albert not only contributed to its cultural and educational agenda but also made generous donations, and together with the Queen, long-term loans, which helped to enrich its burgeoning collection.

The Raphael Collection, on the other hand, had begun in 1853, starting with the vast collections of prints already in the Royal Collection. It then followed with the systematic photography of drawings by Raphael in Windsor Castle and subsequently those in private and public collections in the United Kingdom and abroad. Photographs were paid for by the Prince or exchanged with his own sets.[4] The South Kensington Museum benefited early from this vast enterprise as 52 photographs of Raphael drawings in the Royal Collection were given to the Art Library.[5]

Within this context, Richard Redgrave (1804–1888), who had been made Inspector General for Art at the South Kensington Museum as well as Surveyor of the Queen's Pictures in 1857, organized the photography of

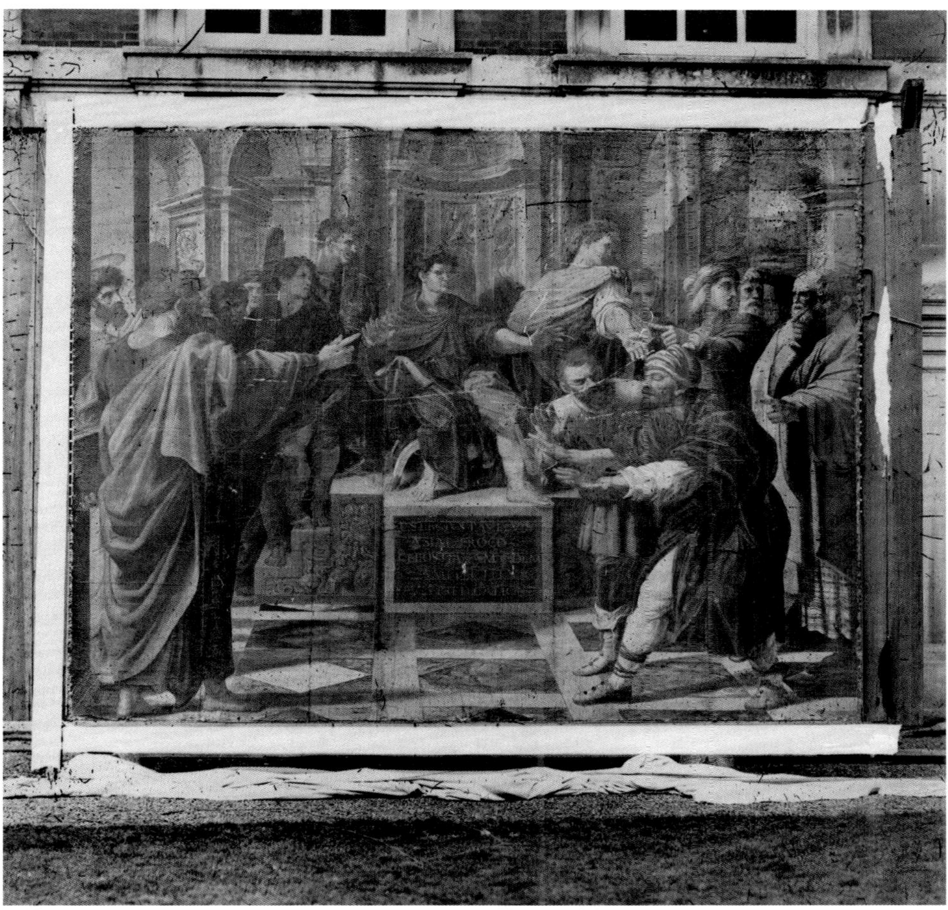

the Raphael Cartoons for the first time in 1858, together with Henry Cole. They were still in Hampton Court Palace and this was not an easy task. Daylight was required and so the Cartoons were carefully removed, through the large windows, into the courtyard to be exposed in the open air (2). This process took several months to complete, given the changing weather conditions and the need to

keep the works safe and dry.[6] The photographer was
Charles Thurston Thompson (1816–1868), who was
already engaged in recording the Raphael Collection
as well as serving as official photographer for the
Department of Science and Art and the South Kensington
Museum. Photography was indeed on the rise as a new
art (and science) but was simultaneously perceived as
a means of obtaining 'specimens of the highest objects
of art at the cheapest possible rate', which could then
be put at the disposal of the public to see or purchase.[7]

Prince Albert and the Royal Librarians Ernst Becker
(1819–1869) and later Carl Ruland (1834–1907) arranged
the collected material (photographs and prints) in large
portfolios, set in an ornate free-standing cabinet in
the Print Room of the Royal Library at Windsor Castle,
where they remain to this day (3).[8] Photographs of the
Cartoons came to form part of the albums numbered 31,
32, 33 and 33a. They also contain prints and photographs
of Raphael's designs relating to the tapestries in the
Sistine Chapel, including reproductions of the tapestries
in the Vatican.

Portfolios of the Raphael
Collection, on display in the
Print Room of the Royal
Library at Windsor Castle

Royal Collection Trust

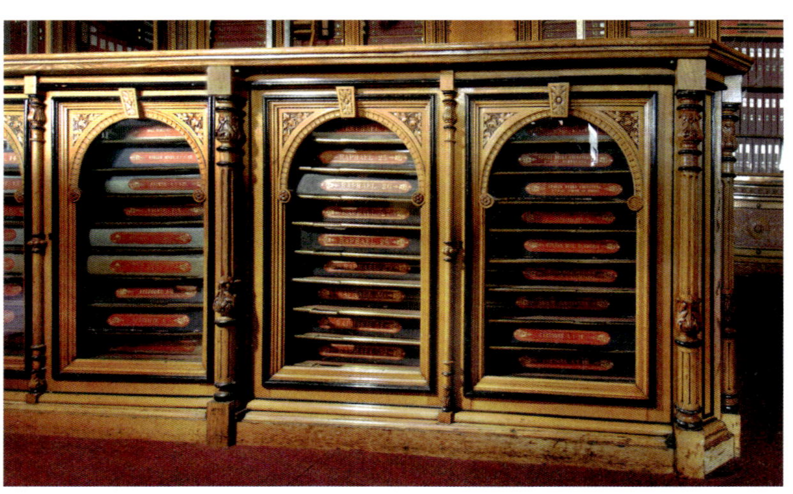

Although specific details of the decision to transfer
the Cartoons to South Kensington remain unknown –
the matter was decided in private between the Queen,
her daughter (the Crown Princess of Prussia) and their
councillors[9] – it seems to have been motivated primarily

'in remembrance of a plan of His Royal Highness the Prince Consort, viz. to assemble together if possible, all Raphael's works now existing in England'.[10] Secondly, permission to move the Cartoons from Hampton Court to the South Kensington Museum was given specifically 'for the use of the students of the schools of art'.[11] Finally, and perhaps more importantly, 'the cartoons were designed for tapestry and most appropriately placed in the South Kensington Museum established to encourage art & manufactures'.[12]

The proximity of Richard Redgrave to the Queen might also have played an important role in this loan. It should be remembered that the Cartoons were, and still are, a personal loan from the monarch. Incidentally the question of the Cartoons' ownership seems to have played no minor role in the unsuccessful pleas the National Gallery addressed to the Queen asking to house the Cartoons in Trafalgar Square. Henry Cole wrote in 1875:

> When Sir C. Eastlake [the National Gallery's first director] applied to Her Majesty to allow the Cartoons to the placed officially in charge of the Trustees of the National Gallery and not of the Lord President of the Council, General Grey told me that this request was refused and that The Queen, considering the Cartoons as possessions of the Crown, peremptorily declined to part with them to the National Gallery. I had some reasons to think that before long another attempt will he make to get the Cartoons into the National Gallery and placed in the near rooms at Charing Cross. So I reminded him of what happened in 1865.[13]

And so the Cartoons were installed in an upper gallery (now Gallery 94) of the South Kensington Museum and were displayed alongside a Mortlake tapestry representing *Christ's Charge to Peter*, as well as other copies after Raphael's work (4). The ambition of this display was to exemplify Prince Albert's idea of presenting the artist's creative process while 'allow[ing] a systematic and complete study of his development'.[14] A proposal for such an exhibition was drawn up by Ruland, who justified the inclusion of reproductions after Raphael's original works so that they 'may be studied most satisfactorily in a faithful engraving, when access to

the distant original is impossible'.[15] However, it was later
felt that such an installation created some confusion
between Raphael's work, namely the Cartoons, and the
copies in various formats and media (5).[16] The relocation
of the Cartoons in their current gallery took place in
1950, following their temporary storage in a specially
constructed shelter during the Second World War.[17]

 This gallery, now known as the Raphael Court,
was not originally designed to house the Cartoons but
was intended for the museum's Indian art collection.
This new setting, however, restored the status of these
works as Renaissance treasures: they were hung alone,

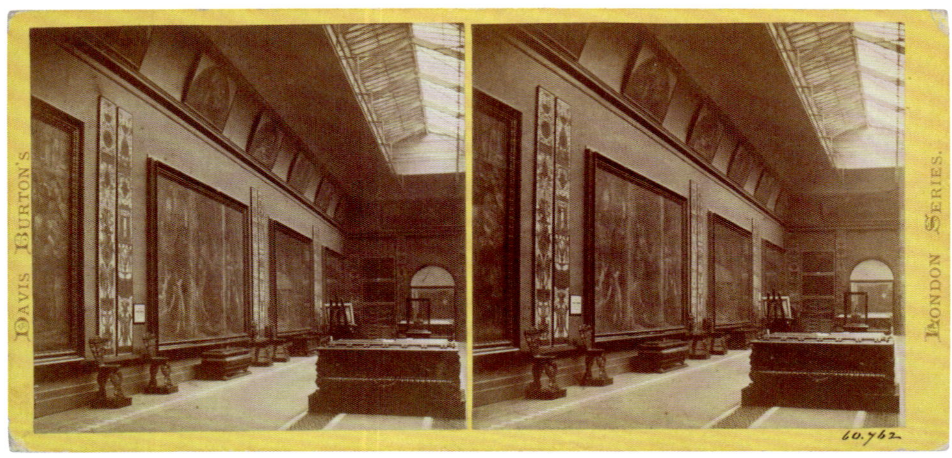

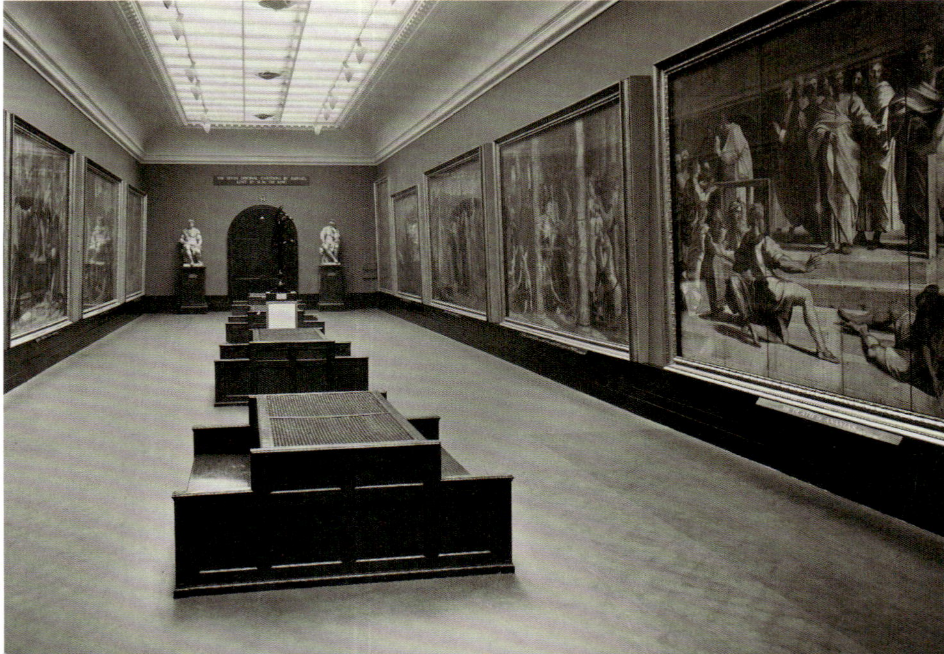

J. Davis Burton
No. 12 in the *London Series*, South
Kensington Museum (Gallery
94), south side showing four of
the Raphael Cartoons, 1868

Stereograph, 8.6 x 17.6 cm
V&A: 60762

The Raphael Cartoons Gallery
(Gallery 94), from the
west end, 1930

Gelatin silver print
V&A: 1924–1932

in conditions similar to those of the tapestries in the
Sistine Chapel. The room itself, incidentally, has virtually
the same dimensions as the papal chapel, only smaller by
two square metres (546 as opposed to 548 square metres).
One Mortlake tapestry, this time representing Raphael's
The Miraculous Draught of Fishes, owned by the Duke of
Buccleuch, was also hung here for comparison to remind
the visitor of the end result of these extraordinary designs.
After a first discrete campaign of restoration in 1964–5,[18]
another phase involving more advanced technical
investigation of the Cartoons was undertaken in the
1990s, from which the current installation results.[19]
However, after more than 25 years, the gallery itself is
in need of renovation. It is therefore to mark the 500th
anniversary of Raphael's death in 2020 that the V&A
has embarked on a major project that takes the
presentation and the didactic apparatus of the Raphael
Cartoons in a whole new direction.

The Cartoons are invaluable examples of a revolution
in design master minded by one of the world's greatest
artists. Raphael's reputation hardly ever waned, unlike
those of many artists whose lifetime success fell quickly
into oblivion after their death. Raphael, on the contrary,
remains at the forefront of artistic training in the
Academies and art-historical studies. However, it was
as a painter that he was chiefly admired, while his work
as a designer, architect and sculptor is still less well
known. The 2020 anniversary offers, therefore, a unique
opportunity to reconsider Raphael's wider oeuvre and
power of invention, as well as his interaction with the
decorative arts that was essential to the artistic world
during the Renaissance. A new approach will consider
questions of connoisseurship, which have occupied the
great part of art history in the last 150 years, as a means
to understand the complex working of such a busy and
successful workshop as Raphael's. The Cartoons highlight
the very specific relationship between the master and his
many gifted assistants. The workshop was also a place
of training, a school before the birth of the Academies,
where the savoir-faire was transmitted, treasured and
subsequently adapted to the ever-evolving taste of the
art market. Our aim is therefore to revive and re-present
this extraordinary laboratory of ideas and craftsmanship
for the enjoyment of all.

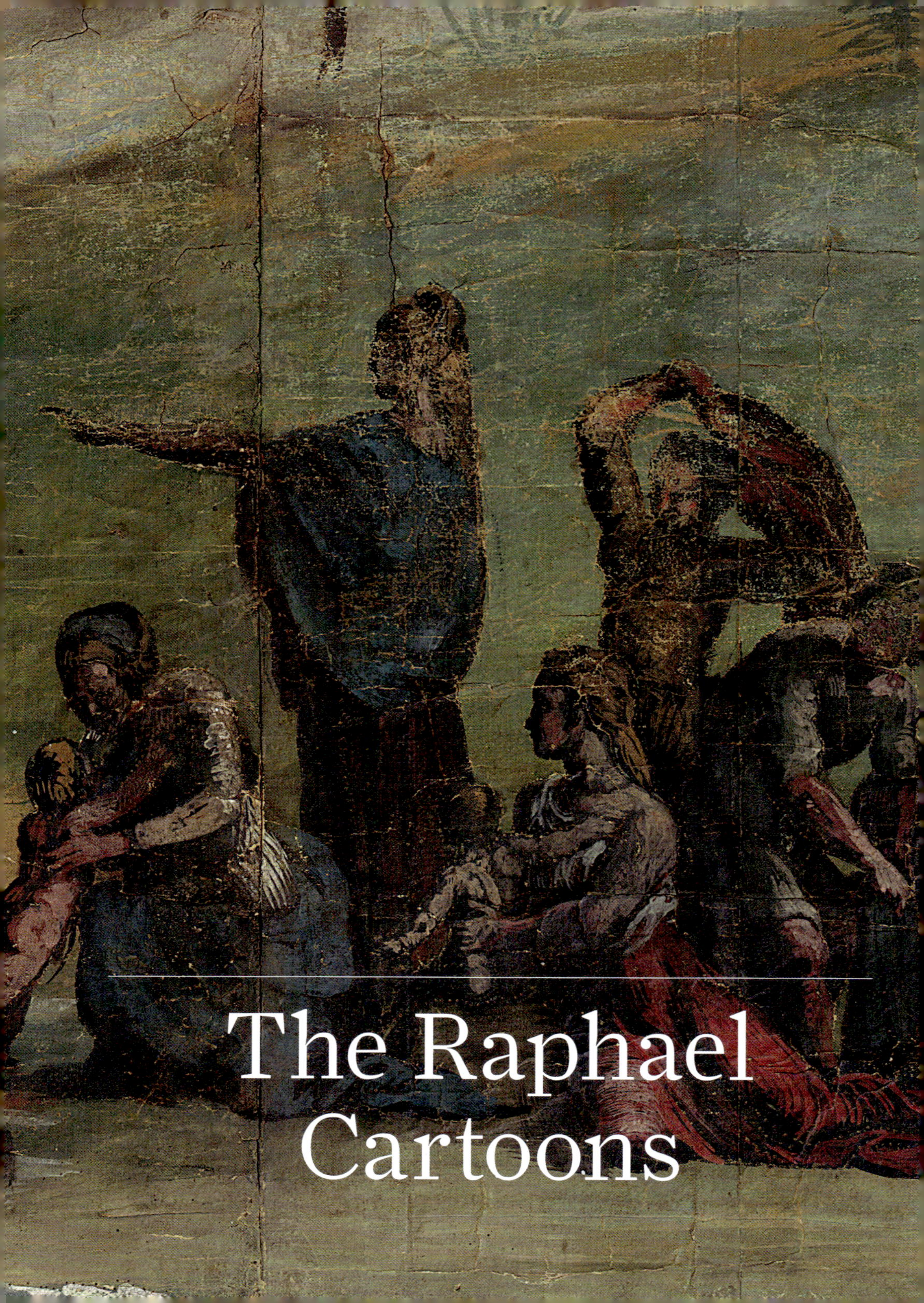

The Raphael Cartoons

Raphael (1483–1520)
The Miraculous Draught of Fishes,
*c.*1515–16
(Luke, 5: 1–10)

Bodycolour over charcoal on paper,
later mounted on canvas in the
17th century, 322 x 401 cm
On loan from Her Majesty
The Queen: RCIN 912944
V&A: ROYAL LOANS.2

Simon (later Peter), Andrew, James and John,
together with their father Zebedee, had been fishing
unsuccessfully in the Lake of Gennesaret (Sea of
Galilee) when Jesus appears and tells Simon to cast
his nets into deep water. Suddenly Simon and his
fellow fishermen make a miraculous catch and their
nets overflow with fish. The story refers to Peter's call
as the first Apostle and future mission as the 'fisher of
men', who converts others to Christianity. It also
demonstrates his humility as he kneels before Christ
in acknowledgement of His divinity.

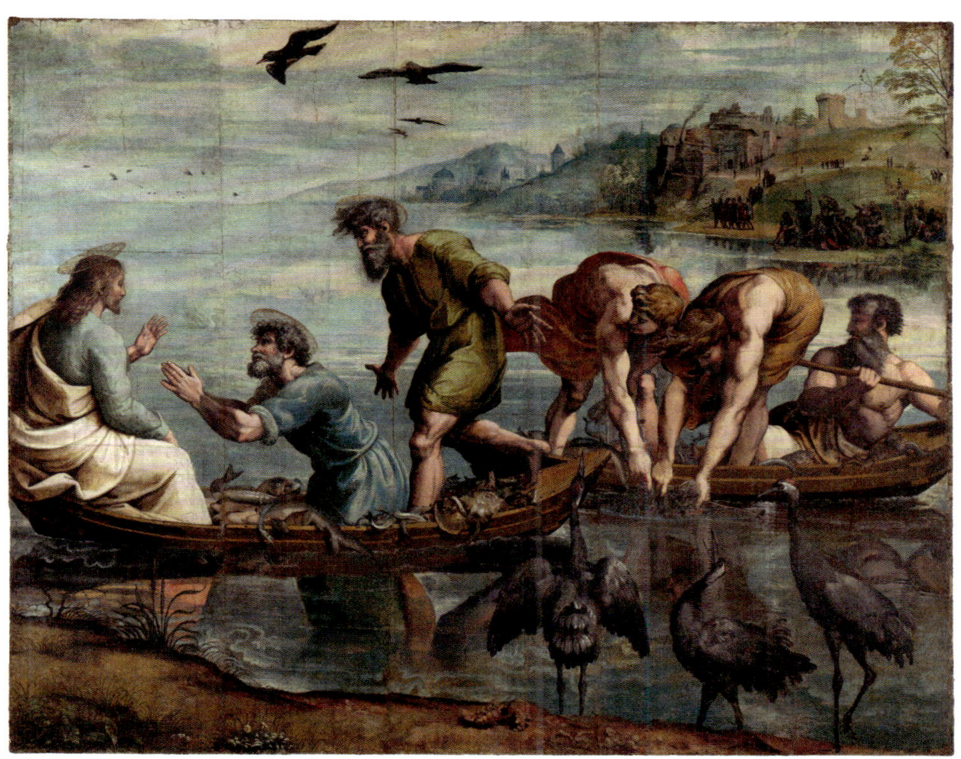

Raphael (1483–1520)
*Christ's Charge to Peter, c.*1515–16
(Matthew, 16: 18–19 and
John, 21: 15–17)

Bodycolour over charcoal on paper,
later mounted on canvas in the
17th century, 344 x 534 cm
On loan from Her Majesty
The Queen: RCIN 912945
V&A: ROYAL LOANS.3

This scene combines two stories described in the Gospels of Matthew and John to illustrate Peter's pivotal role in the Christian Church. After the Resurrection, Christ addresses the Apostles and charges Peter with the care of the faithful, symbolized by the sheep, and gives him the keys of the Gates of Heaven. Peter is made the foundation stone of the Church, and Christ's successor on earth.

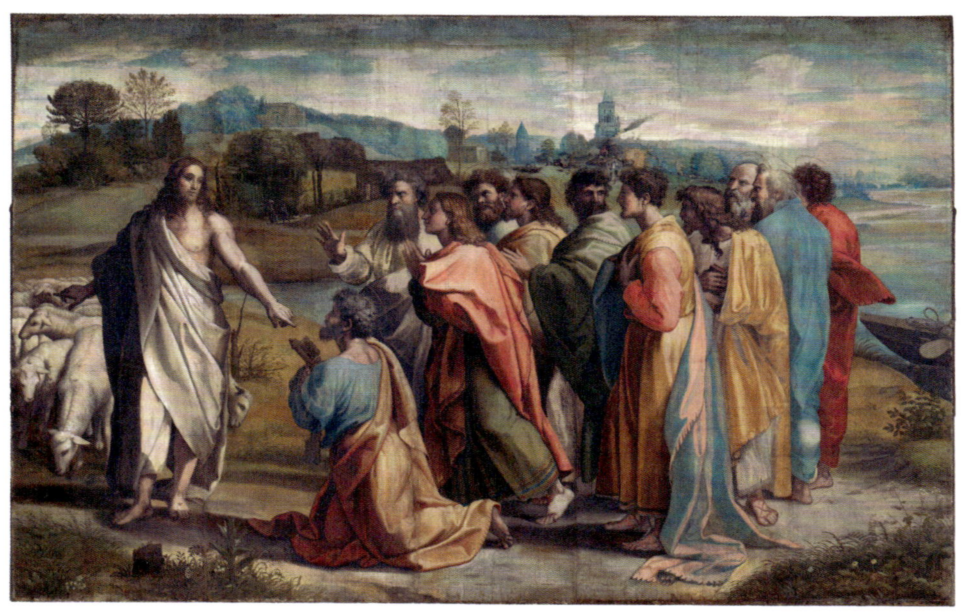

8

Raphael (1483–1520)
The Healing of the Lame Man,
c.1515–16
(Acts, 3: 1–8)

Bodycolour over charcoal on paper,
later mounted on canvas in the
17th century, 345 x 537 cm
On loan from Her Majesty
The Queen: RCIN 912946
V&A: ROYAL LOANS.4

At the Beautiful Gate of the Temple of Jerusalem, among the crowd, Peter heals a lame man, a miracle that symbolizes Peter's spiritual healing. Next to Peter stands John the Evangelist, who looks on. The twisted columns are based on antique examples in St Peter's Cathedral, then thought to have come from Solomon's Temple in Jerusalem.

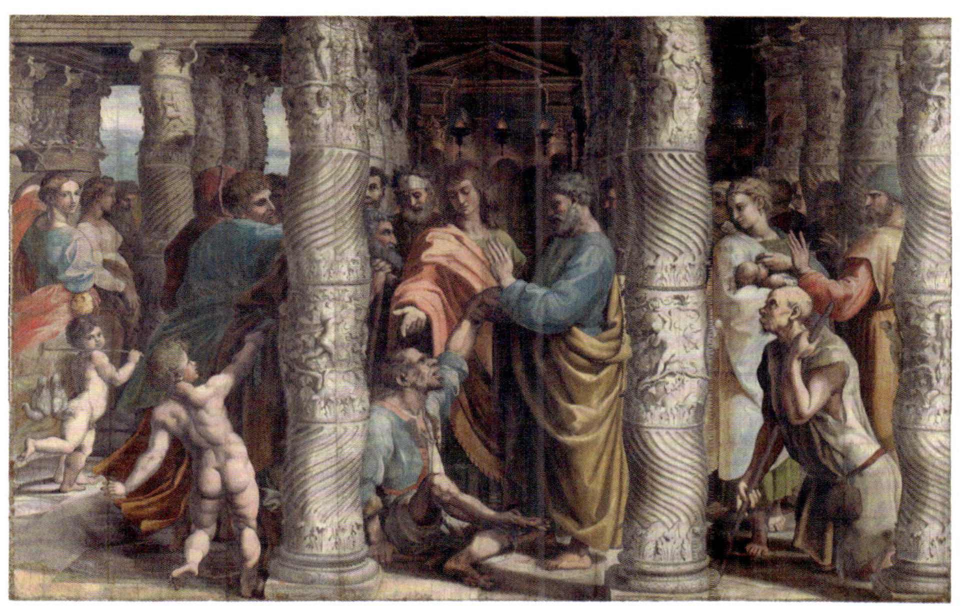

Raphael (1483–1520)
The Death of Ananias, c.1515–16
(Acts, 5: 1–5)

Bodycolour over charcoal on paper,
later mounted on canvas in the
17th century, 343 x 530 cm
On loan from Her Majesty
The Queen: RCIN 912947
V&A: ROYAL LOANS.5

In this scene the Apostles have persuaded some men to sell off some property so that the proceeds can be distributed among the poor. One of them, Ananias, secretly keeps back some of the proceeds for himself. Peter rebukes Ananias for his deceitfulness, and Ananias falls down dead.

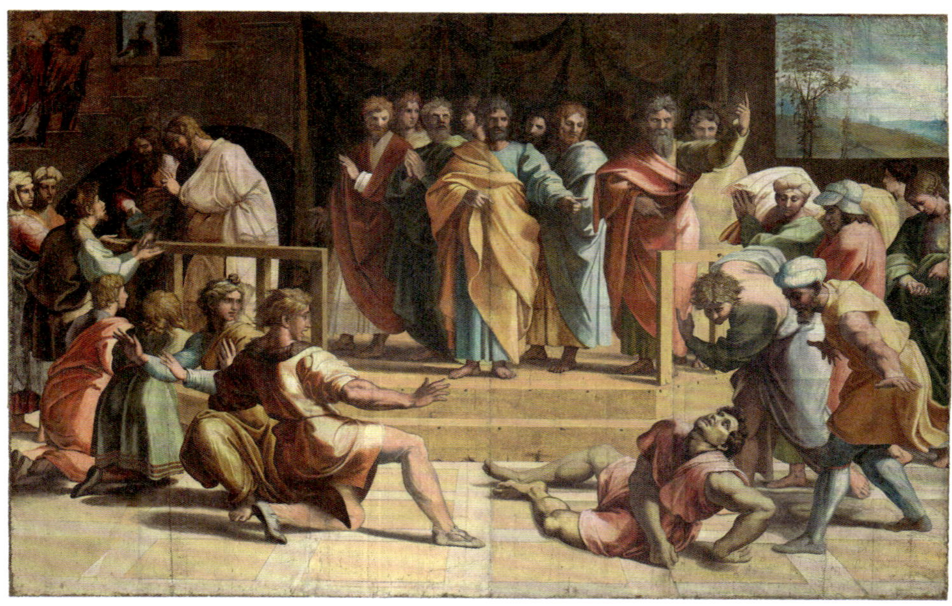

Raphael (1483–1520)
The Conversion of the Proconsul,
c.1515–16
(Acts, 13:6–12)

Bodycolour over charcoal on paper,
later mounted on canvas in the
17th century, 344 x 446 cm
On loan from Her Majesty
The Queen: RCIN 912948
V&A: ROYAL LOANS.8

The sorcerer Elymas has tried to prevent Paul and
Barnabas from converting the Roman proconsul
Sergius Paulus to Christianity. Paul strikes him blind
temporarily. Witnessing this, the proconsul
embraces the Christian faith. The story illustrates
Paul's mission to convert the Gentiles, while Peter's
vocation is to convert the Jews.

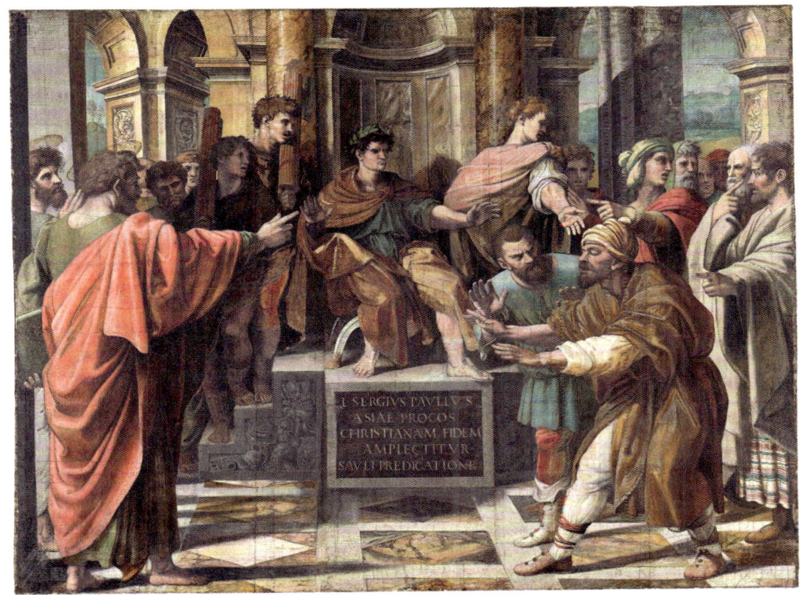

Raphael (1483–1520)
The Sacrifice at Lystra, *c.*1515–16
(Acts, 14:8–18)

Bodycolour over charcoal on paper,
later mounted on canvas in the
17th century, 342 x 540 cm
On loan from Her Majesty
The Queen: RCIN 912949
V&A: ROYAL LOANS.6

Paul and Barnabas heal a lame man in the city
of Lystra (now Hatunsaray in modern Turkey).
The inhabitants of Lystra then mistake Paul and
Barnabas for the local gods Jupiter and Mercury and,
following tradition, prepare to offer them a sacrifice.
Paul tears his clothes in dismay, while Barnabas tries
to stop the sacrifice, admonishing the Lystrians for
their idolatry.

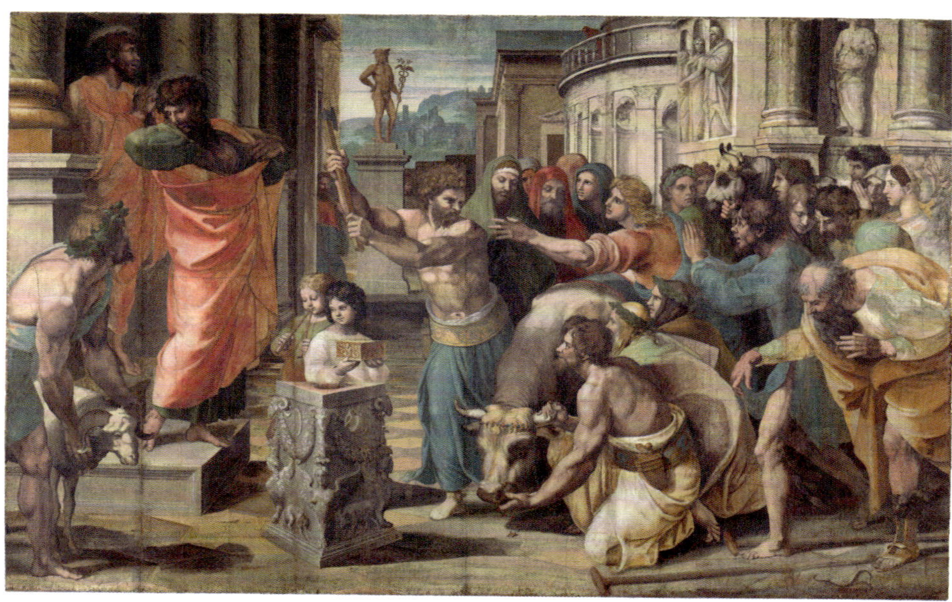

Raphael (1483–1520)
*Paul Preaching at Athens, c.*1515–16
(Acts, 17: 16–34)

Bodycolour over charcoal on paper,
later mounted on canvas in the
17th century, 343 x 443 cm
On loan from Her Majesty
The Queen: RCIN 912950
V&A: ROYAL LOANS.7

Paul stands in the Agora in Athens and preaches on the immortality of the soul before a group of men including ancient philosophers. The crowd is captured in a range of attitudes from attention and surprise to scepticism. The man wearing a red bonnet behind Paul has been identified as a possible portrait of Pope Leo X.

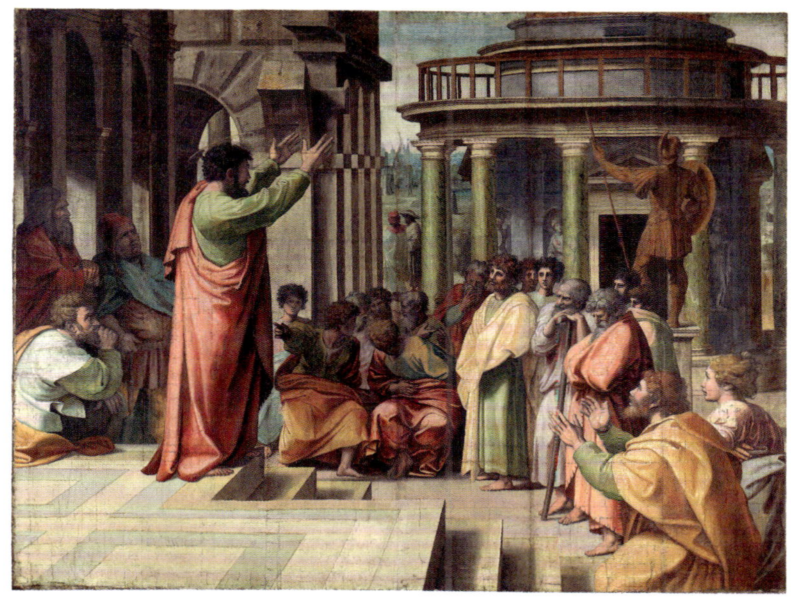

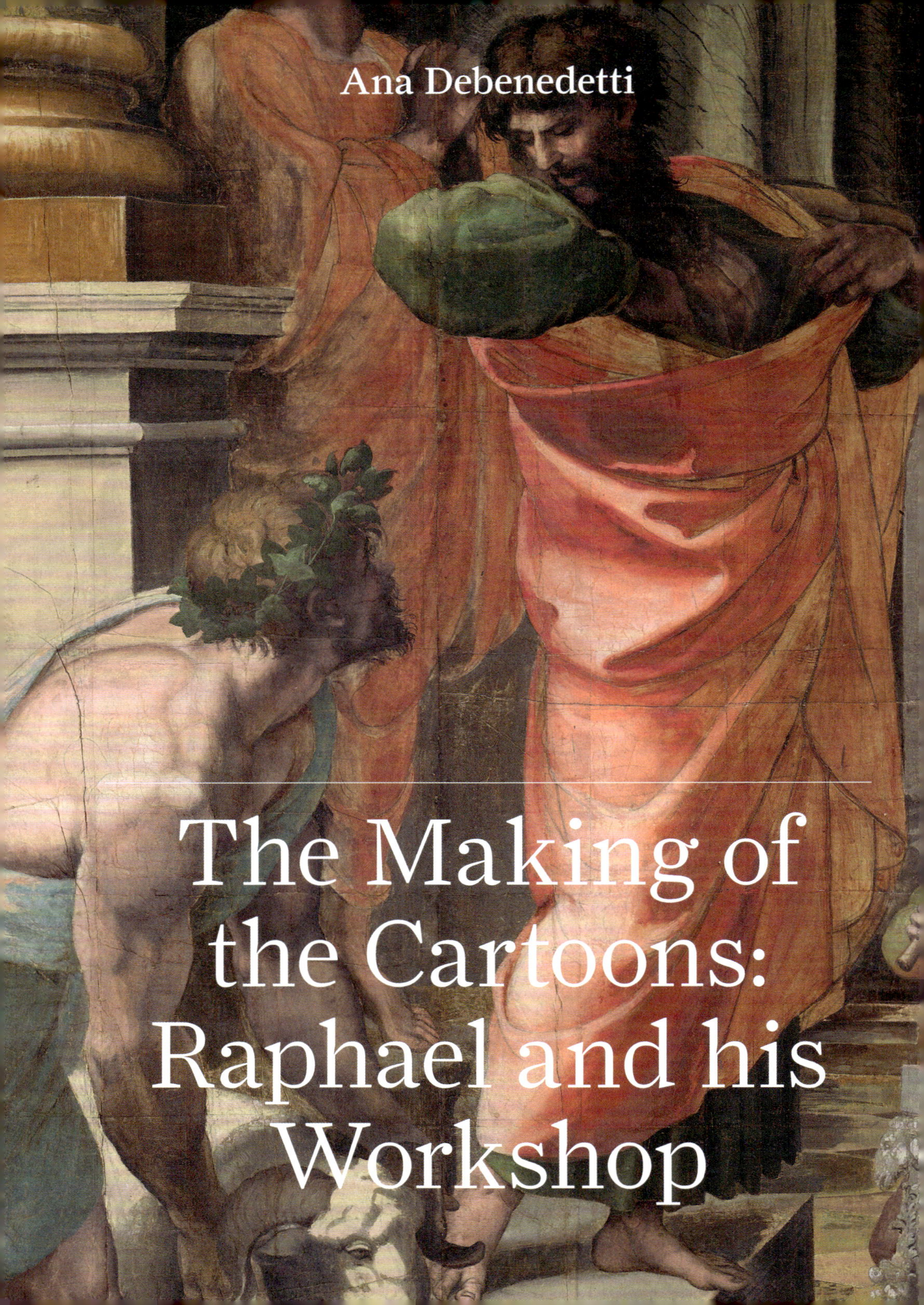

The Making of the Cartoons: Raphael and his Workshop

No works of art in the Renaissance were created without
a purpose. The Raphael Cartoons would not exist
without the man who originally commissioned them
and the important site for which they were devised.
Elected in 1513 to the highest position in the hierarchy
of the Christian church, Pope Leo X (Giovanni de' Medici,
r.1513–21), the son of Lorenzo the Magnificent, was heir
to a dynasty with an active role in the patronage of the
arts. He therefore naturally wanted to make his own
contribution to the ornamentation of the Vatican Palace
in Rome, and specifically the private papal chapel.
Consequently, the large designs known today as the
Raphael Cartoons, now in the V&A, were therefore
commissioned for a specific site and purpose from Pope
Leo's favourite: the Urbino-born Raffaello Santi, better
known as Raphael (1483–1520).

Since the Middle Ages, the Vatican Palace (the papal
residence) and the adjacent Basilica of St Peter had
undergone many campaigns of refurbishment and
embellishment, which culminated in the destruction
and rebuilding of the Basilica under Pope Julius II
(Giuliano della Rovere, r.1503–13). One of the holiest places
in Christendom, the Basilica was allegedly erected over
the burial site of the first bishop of Rome, and thus the
first pope, St Peter. A decisive milestone was reached in
the Vatican Palace in the 1470s, when it was decided to
reconfigure the papal chapel built by Pope Nicholas III
(Giovanni Gaetano Orsini, r.1277–80). The new chapel
was erected in 1473–81 for Pope Sixtus IV (Francesco della
Rovere, r.1471–84), who gave it his name ('Sistine' derives
from 'Sixtus').

As soon as the chapel was completed, Sixtus IV,
following tradition, commissioned a scheme of fresco
decoration that would cover the entire surface of the
chapel's walls. He summoned a group of leading artists
including two Florentine painters, Sandro Botticelli
(1444/5–1510) and Domenico Ghirlandaio (1449–1494),
as well as the Tuscan Luca Signorelli (1450–1523) and the
Umbrian Pietro Perugino (1446–1523), Raphael's future
master. They painted the middle register of the lateral
walls with a series of frescoes depicting the Life of Christ
on one side and the Life of Moses on the other, beneath
a row of full-length niched figures representing the
pre-Constantinian Popes. This first phase of decoration
was completed for the feast of the Assumption of the

Virgin (to whom the chapel is dedicated), celebrated on 15 August 1483. Pope Sixtus IV died the following year and after a 20-year transition, during which three popes reigned, Sixtus' nephew, Pope Julius II, was elected in 1503. It was he who commissioned Michelangelo (1475–1564) to paint the famous ceiling frescoes with scenes from the Book of Genesis and figures of the Sibyls and Prophets (1508–12). When Leo X came to power in 1513, there were few spaces left in the chapel for him to make his own artistic intervention (13). However, the lower register of the lateral walls was frescoed with a *trompe l'oeil* decoration of simulated non-figurative hangings (14).[1] It was this relatively 'free' space that prompted him to commission a series of tapestries to be hung, on special occasions, in place of the painted ones.

'The Pope desired to have rich tapestry hangings of gold and silk.'

Vasari, 1568 [2]

By 1515 Raphael had already accomplished the decoration of two rooms in the Vatican Palace, the Stanza della Segnatura and the Stanza d'Eliodoro, both commissioned by Julius II and completed respectively in 1511 and 1514.[3] At this point Raphael was at the peak of his career, and one of the most celebrated artists in Europe. According to Vasari, Pope Leo X was so impressed with Raphael's achievements that he commissioned him to design the ten tapestries intended to ornament the Sistine Chapel.[4] Leo X probably thought these would be the final element in the decoration of the Chapel; however, a quarter-century later, in 1541, Michelangelo completed *The Last Judgement*, a vast fresco covering the whole altar wall, replacing Perugino's original frescoed altarpiece and two of the original fifteenth-century narrative scenes. Michelangelo's achievement, therefore, became the very last contribution to the decorative scheme of the Sistine Chapel.

Raphael's tapestry designs were specifically made to complement the Chapel's fifteenth-century frescoes and are an extraordinary testimony to his artistic versatility and power of invention. The creative and executive

⌣ 13

Antonio de' Benintendi (?)
Bust of Cardinal Giovanni
de' Medici, the future
Pope Leo X, *c.*1512

Polychrome terracotta, H. 38.5 cm
V&A: A.29–1982

process occupied Raphael between June 1515 and
December 1516, a period that corresponds to the first
and last payments he received for this commission.[5]
The set was to represent the lives of St Peter and St Paul,
traditionally considered as the founding fathers of the
Christian church; hence its series title, the Acts of the
Apostles. The iconography was devised by members of
the papal court while the compositions themselves were
left to the artist. Raphael was particularly favoured as he
excelled in translating complex ideas and propagandistic
messages into clear, simple and harmonious ensembles.
Furthermore, Raphael was supremely versatile visually
and intellectually, very necessary as he had not only to
comply with the style of the earlier frescoes but also to
conceive a series whose narrative would clearly relate to
the scenes above. A further challenge was to anticipate
the transformation of his designs, which would be woven
as mirror images of his originals by means of the low-
warp loom technique employed in the Netherlands.

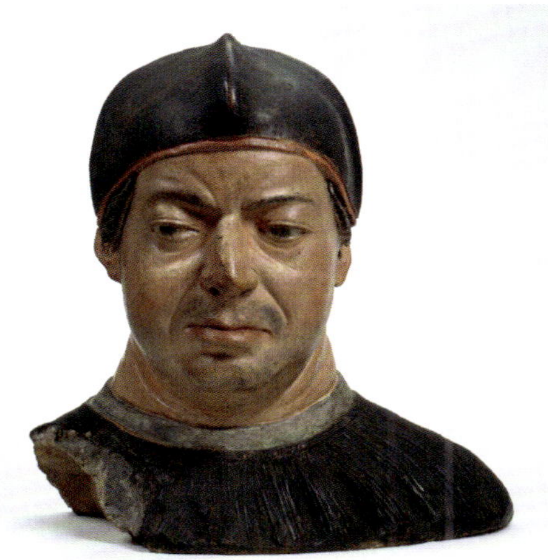

Raphael's compositions re-affirm the authority of the
Pope as the legitimate heir of the first Bishop of Rome
and vicar of Jesus Christ on earth. Four scenes illustrate
episodes from the life of St Peter (the Petrine cycle),
namely *The Miraculous Draught of Fishes*, *Christ's Charge
to Peter*, *The Healing of the Lame Man* and *The Death of
Ananias*, while six are devoted to the life of St Paul (the
Pauline cycle): *The Stoning of Stephen*, *The Conversion of
Saul*, *The Conversion of the Proconsul* (also called *The*

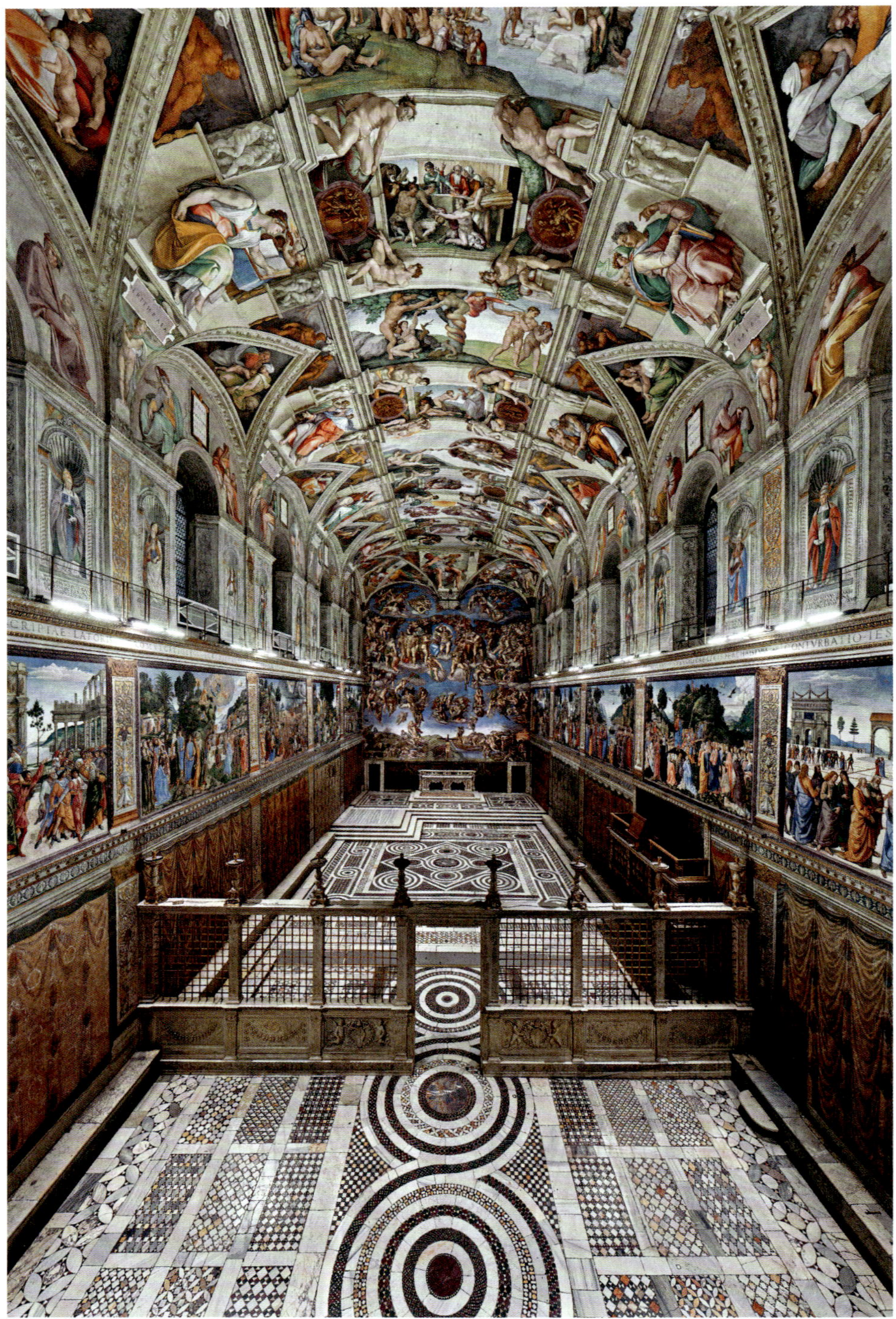

Blinding of Elymas), *The Sacrifice at Lystra*, *Paul in Prison* and *Paul Preaching at Athens*. All were surrounded with borders: the bottom edge illustrates scenes from the life of Leo X for the Petrine cycle, and from the life of St Paul for the Pauline cycle; the lateral borders show allegories of the Seven Liberal Arts, the Seven Virtues, the Hours, the Seasons, the Elements and the Labours of Hercules. No Cartoons of the borders have survived and only seven out of the ten original Cartoons came to the V&A. The lost Cartoons are *The Stoning of Stephen*, *The Conversion of Saul* and *Paul in Prison*, now only known through the surviving tapestries.

'[Raphael] made in appropriate form and size, of his own hand [*di sua mano*], the coloured cartoons, which were sent to Flanders to be woven.'

Vasari, 1568 [6]

Tapestries are not created directly onto the loom. Instead a designer provides a template in the form of a full-sized drawing for the weaver to follow. The traditional process of tapestry-making implied then (and still does today) a division of labour between an artist-designer who conceives and draws the composition and a weaver who translates the design into a woven textile. The composition is supplied in the form of full-scale preparatory drawings, usually (but not exclusively) executed on paper, hence their name *cartone* (big paper) in Italian, derived from *carta*, paper, and translated as 'cartoon' in English. The making of cartoons was a common practice throughout the Middle Ages and the Renaissance. They were especially employed for fresco decorations, but also for the decorative arts (embroidery, marquetry and mosaics). The destructive process of transferring the design onto the final support explains why very few have survived, and when they do, it is usually in a fragmentary form. Thus the seven extant tapestry Cartoons by Raphael comprise a unique Renaissance treasure, both in terms of aesthetic value and technical achievement.

In his long introduction on artistic techniques to the *Lives of the Most Excellent Painters, Sculptors, and Architects* (first published in 1550 and in a revised and augmented edition in 1568), Giorgio Vasari (1511–1574), one of the first art historians, describes the process whereby a composition is first born in the artist's mind and then translated into an initial rapid sketch on paper (*schizzo*). This notional idea is further refined in a small drawing described as a 'blot drawing' (*macchia*). A series of more finished drawings (*disegni*) perfects the design. When the composition has reached a satisfactory resolution, it is transferred onto a larger, full-scale support, the cartoon (*cartone*). Large cartoons are traditionally made up of several sheets of paper glued together with flour paste and boiled water (*colla di farina*

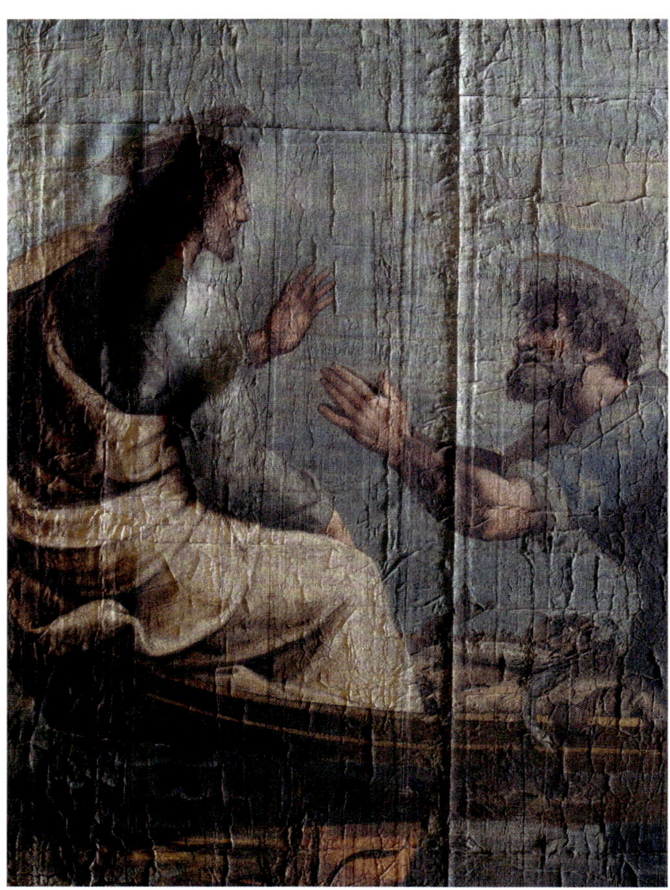

≈ **15**

Raphael (1483–1520)
The Miraculous Draught of Fishes
(detail photographed in
raking light)

*e acqua cotta al fuoc*o). They are then hung by the edges against the wall in order to facilitate the transfer to them of the small finished design.[7] Hardly distinguishable with the naked eye, the joins between the many sheets of paper that make up each of Raphael's Cartoons are clearly apparent when photographed in raking light (15). Each cartoon is composed of nearly 200 sheets of paper, with overall dimensions ranging from 420–30 millimetres in height by 285–90 millimetres in width, which broadly corresponds to a standard Renaissance *reale* paper size, cut in half.[8]

Raphael did not work on such a colossal project alone. He had a team of collaborators to assist him with the different phases of the design process, including the physical assembling of the cartoon itself. A number of preparatory drawings have survived and are now scattered among various public and private collections (there are three in the Royal Collection).[9] These range from first ideas (*schizzi*) to finished compositions (*disegni*), to use Vasari's nomenclature. Typically, different hands can be identified in these many drawings, but Raphael certainly drew most of them; they record his exploration of compositional ideas, placement of the figures and facial expressions. He was probably also responsible for the execution of some of the final presentation drawings (*modelli*); that for *The Conversion of the Proconsul* is entirely autograph (16).[10]

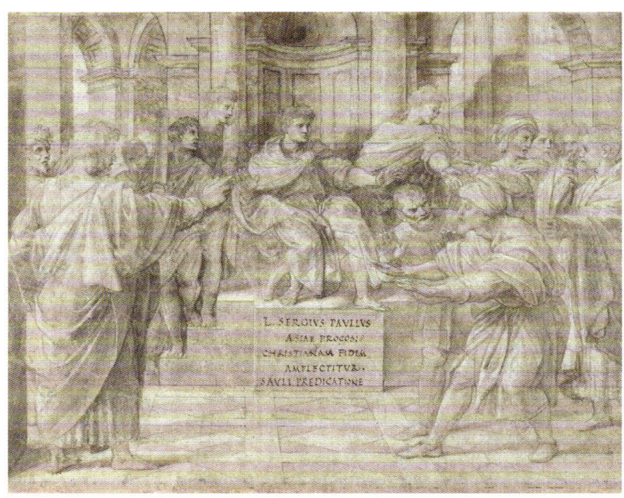

<< 15

Raphael (1483–1520)
Modello for *The Conversion of the Proconsul*, c.1515

Metalpoint, brown wash and white heightening on prepared paper, 26.9 x 35.4 cm
Royal Collection Trust:
RCIN 912750, RL12750

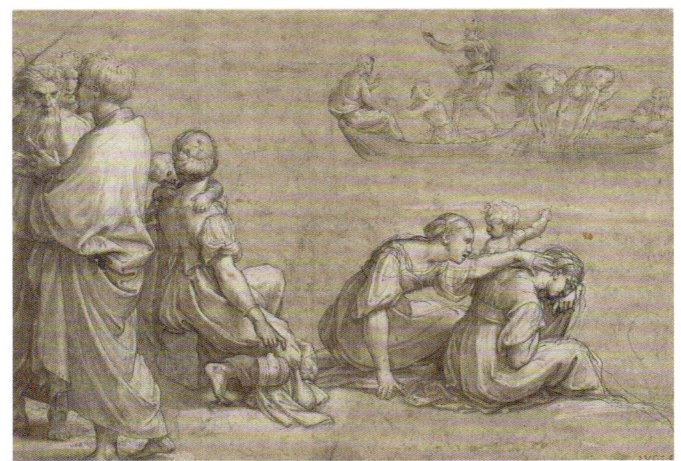

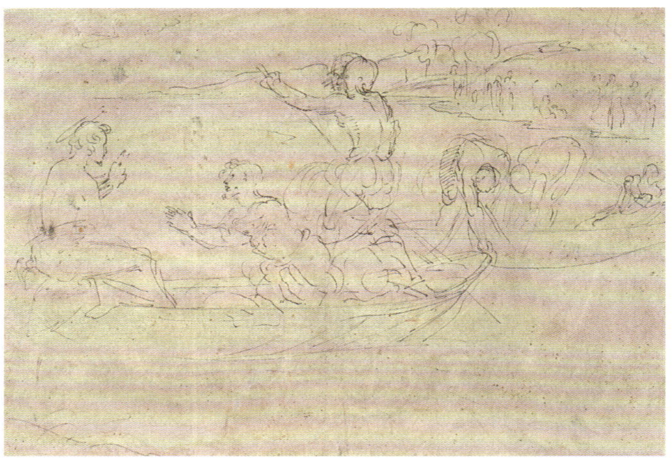

The compositions for which the largest number of drawings has survived are the first two Cartoons, namely *The Miraculous Draught of Fishes* and *Christ's Charge to Peter*. Although there is no surviving *modello* for the former, the preparatory studies provide an interesting insight into the master's creative process. It seems that Raphael initially planned to reverse the traditional arrangement by placing the main event in the background, and bringing forward a secondary, anecdotal scene into the foreground. This first idea is shown on the recto of a drawing in the Albertina, Vienna, which depicts Christ, the fishermen and their boats in the distance while a group of women and children, flanked on one side by standing men, occupies the foreground (17).[11] A study

Raphael (1483–1520)
Studies for The Miraculous
Draught of Fishes *(recto
and verso),* c.1515

Pen, brush and brown ink, brown
wash with white heightening over
black chalk on paper, 22.9 x 32.7 cm
Albertina, Vienna: 192r. and v.

∨ 19

Attributed to Raphael (1483–1520)
Study for The Miraculous Draught
of Fishes, *c.*1514

Pen and ink, wash and lead-white
bodycolour, over black and red chalk,
on washed paper, 20 x 33.9 cm
Royal Collection Trust:
RCIN 912749

of a woman with an outstretched arm confirms that this option was pursued for some time before Raphael decided (or was advised) to go back to a more traditional scheme.[12] The subsequent rearrangement of the figures stresses the importance for Raphael of producing a clear and easily accessible narrative. By pushing the main scene into the background, Raphael might have confused his audience. Hence, on the verso of the same sheet, he rapidly sketched the outlines of what would become the definitive configuration (18). This sketch may correspond to what Vasari describes as a *schizzo* or *macchia*, which allows for the fixing of the prime idea before refining the design further.[13] With this second solution, Raphael enhanced the clarity of his composition by opting for a unity of time, place and action hardly seen in tapestry design before. In addition, as the tapestries were intended to be hung in close proximity to members of the clergy, the placing of imposing figures in the foreground, with a restrained perspective, would have contrasted positively with the frescoes above, which abound in perspectival effects. This new solution undoubtedly provides a better articulation of the whole ensemble. A further study shows this subsequent phase of development (19).[14]

In refining his design, Raphael would also use the members of his workshop as occasional sitters. This typical workshop strategy can be seen in two preparatory studies: a red chalk drawing, which only survives in

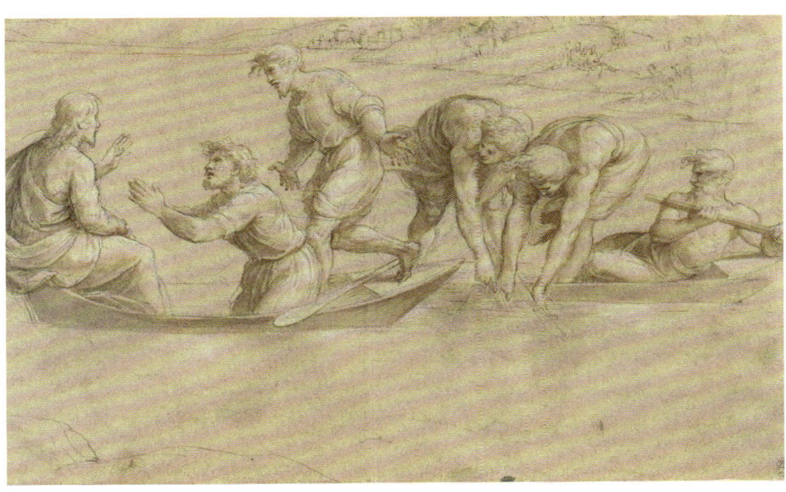

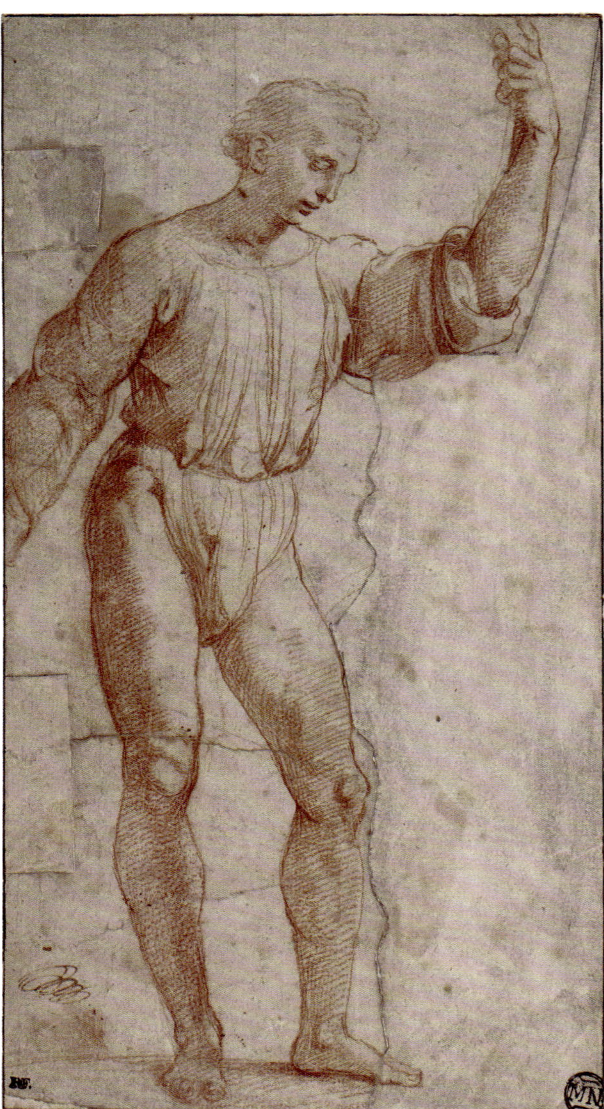

three fragments, for *Christ's Charge to Peter* (**20**, **21**) and a painterly drawing for *The Sacrifice at Lystra* (**22**).[15] In these studies members of the workshop, wearing contemporary clothes, assumed the pose of the biblical protagonists so that the master could study the relationship between the figures and their disposition in space. A counterproof (that is, a reverse impression) of the red chalk drawing,

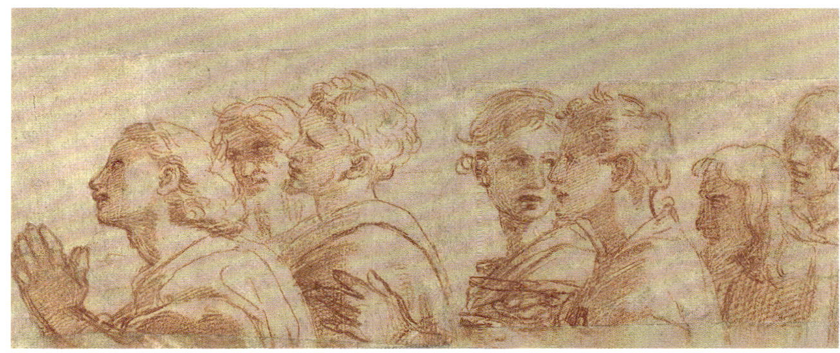

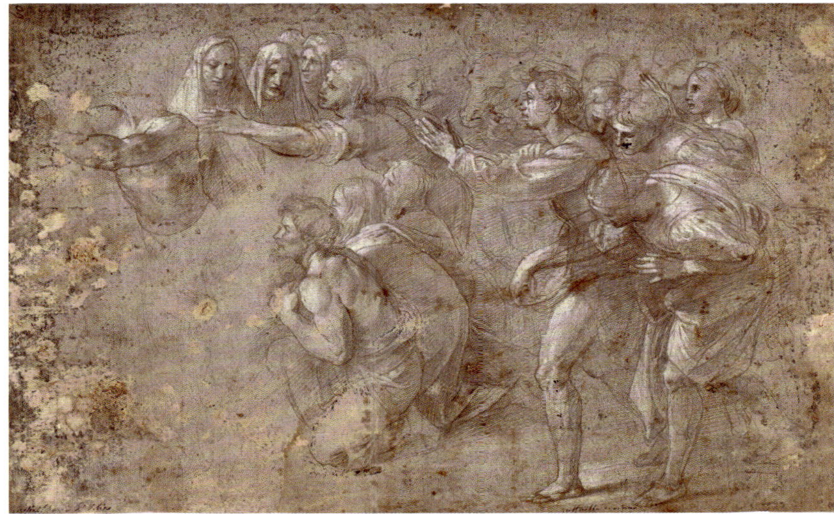

made when it was still complete, records its original
appearance; it was probably made to explore the final
effect of the composition, which would appear as a
mirror image in the tapestry.[16]

The role of members of the workshop was not
limited to acting as occasional sitters. Raphael also
delegated some phases of the design process itself to
one or more assistants, working from a sequence of
detailed preliminary studies by the master. This can be
seen in a drawing for *Paul Preaching at Athens*, attributed
to his collaborator and pupil Giovan Francesco Penni
(*c*.1490–1528) who seems to have been much used by
Raphael in a 'secretarial' role to make modelli.[17] A study
of birds attributed to Giovanni da Udine (1487–1564), who,
according to Vasari, excelled at representing animals,

37

was doubtless executed in preparation for the many birds (cranes, ravens and swans) that inhabit the final version of the first design of *The Miraculous Draught of Fishes*.[18] This delegation of tasks extended to various parts of the Cartoons themselves, in which different hands can be observed. Vasari reports that Penni 'proved of great assistance to Raphael in painting the majority of the Cartoons for the hangings of the Pope's chapel … especially the borders [*fregiature*]'.[19]

Many other people must have assisted the master. Giulio Romano (*c*.1492/99–1546), who joined Raphael's workshop in about 1516, probably also contributed to this vast enterprise. Vasari further describes Raphael's team as a family of artists and notes with admiration how these strong characters worked in harmony under Raphael's supervision. Today the identification of the contributions of Raphael's assistants in these typical collaborative works is still subject to debate but it seems all the more extraordinary, in the light of this culture of collaboration, that Raphael personally contributed so much to the execution of the Cartoons. Vasari informs us that Raphael 'made in appropriate form and size, of his own hand [*di sua mano*], the coloured cartoons, which were sent to Flanders to be woven'.[20] Although it was Raphael's practice to create his own cartoons for easel paintings and frescoes, it was quite rare for an artist of his status to execute such large tapestry designs personally, as it was time-consuming and labour-intensive. Traditionally, a specialist would take care of enlarging the small final drawing onto the full-scale cartoon.[21] In this case, Raphael probably did so in part because he was aware that he would not be able to supervise the production of the tapestries, which were to be woven in Brussels in the workshop of Pieter van Aelst (*c*.1450–1533), the leading merchant-weaver at the time. Raphael's degree of personal involvement might also have been the consequence of some anxiety about designing for a medium – tapestry (less subtle than fresco painting) – in which he had not previously worked.

The division of labour is key to understanding the working principles and dynamic structure of the Renaissance workshop. Large workshops such as Raphael's produced a wide variety of artworks at an extremely rapid pace. Delegation, collaboration and assistance within the workshop were the only way to deliver such a large number of works within the tight time frame imposed by the commissions. Indeed, by 1515 Raphael had completed the frescoes of two large rooms in the Vatican Palace and was already engaged in decorating the walls of the Stanza dell'Incendio.

The following year, while apparently fully dedicated to the creation of the Sistine tapestry cartoons, Raphael conceived a decorative scheme for the personal apartments of Cardinal Bibbiena (1470–1520) in the Vatican Palace, specifically the bathroom (*Stufetta*) and the corridor (*Loggetta*), which were painted by his team, in addition to completing several important easel paintings.[22] At that time, he was a so probably working out the decorative scheme for the large corridor space of Leo X's private quarters (*Logge*), which he supervised, although it was effectively completed in 1518–19 by his most gifted pupils: Giulio Romano and Giovan Francesco Penni. During those years, Raphael also continued his work as an architect. In 1514 he succeeded Bramante (1444–1514) in the role of Architect of the Basilica of St Peter and, among other projects, submitted designs for the facade of the Basilica of San Lorenzo (1515–16), the Medici church in Florence, as well as the papal residence, now known as Villa Madama.[23]

Vasari gives perhaps the most comprehensive account of Raphael's workshop strategy when describing the execution of the frescoes that adorned the Vatican *Logge*, completed just after the Sistine Cartoons. While Raphael himself concentrated on the overall design, his large team proceeded to the transfer and painting of the scenes on the pilasters and vaults.

> Raphael prepared the designs for the stucco ornaments and the scenes painted there, as well as of the borders. He appointed Giovanni da Udine head of the stucco and grotesque work, and Giulio Romano of the figures [...]. Gio Francesco, also il Bologna, Perino del Vaga, Pellegrino da Modana, Vincenzo da S. Gimignano, and Polidoro da Caravaggio, with many other painters, did scenes and figures and other things for that work [...].[24]

This description gives us an idea of the different kinds of team helping Raphael to translate his designs and execute the multi-faceted aspects of his decorative schemes; the modern equivalent might be a team creating the decor of a theatrical stage. The Renaissance concept of authorship was not compromised by this collaborative work; in fact, as Vasari explains in the life of Giulio Romano, 'if the work is retouched by the artist, it is therefore his'.[25]

Raphael's Cartoons embody a true revolution in tapestry design, blurring the boundaries between painting and weaving.

His great innovation lay in his conception of tapestry designs as vast woven frescoes, an approach that diverged significantly from previous tradition. The scale, drama and arrangement of the Cartoons were inspired in part by the large-scale mural decorations of the Vatican Stanze he had just completed and direct quotations from this ensemble can be observed in the Cartoons. Other aspects echo the art of Masaccio (1401–*c*.1428) and Filippino Lippi (1457–1504) in the Brancacci Chapel in Florence among others, and the monuments and artefacts from ancient Rome.[26] Raphael's creation took the medium of tapestry in an entirely new direction and greatly influenced the next generation, especially Netherlandish artists such as Bernard von Orley (1487–1541) and Pieter Coecke van Aelst (1502–1550).[27] Similarly, Giulio Romano and Perino del Vaga (1501–1547), Raphael's artistic heirs, perpetuated and developed further their master's new formula in their own creations, as can be seen from their own surviving tapestry designs for the palaces of Mantua and Genoa.[28]

For the first time, a series of tapestries, which were traditionally conceived as moveable luxury goods and had the flexibility to be arranged differently each time according to the venue, had been created for a specific site. It is generally believed that they were originally made for a particular hanging within the Sistine Chapel, given their various dimensions, specific light sources (which respectively alternate from left to right) and sequential narrative order. What this original sequence was remains a long-standing debate.[29] It is certain that Raphael's designs cannot be fully understood outside the grand decorative scheme of the Chapel. They were created to be placed below the Quattrocento frescoes that covered the middle register of the Chapel, including the altar wall, and originally included 16 scenes, inserted within a system of fictive pilasters and entablatures. The extraordinary conservation of the Cartoons, and especially of their pigments, reveals that Raphael used the same acidic, cool palette as the Quattrocento frescoes in an attempt to link the two programmes chromatically. This homogeneous palette would have enhanced the role and status of the tapestries, stylistically conceived as a structural base (*basamento*) for the episodes from the lives of Christ and Moses located above. In this respect, with their large figures solidly settled in the foreground and their clear narrative, the tapestries would have drawn the spectator's eyes to the upper level. This chromatic harmony is now unfortunately easily missed, since the tapestries themselves have lost their original splendour due to the inevitable fading of natural pigments over time, exacerbated by their regular use for nearly five centuries. Today, the original appearance of the tapestries can only be judged by looking at the reverse, where the precious and delicate silk and wool have retained some of their intense pigmentation.

This context explains the high degree of finish of the Cartoons and the care Raphael took in painting them, which was more extensive than generally deemed necessary for tapestry cartoons. Most of the full-scale tapestry cartoons that have survived show a much thinner paint layer and lightly coloured washes. However, from the beginning of the sixteenth century, highly finished, generally monochrome, cartoons were increasingly being produced as preparatory designs for frescoes and easel paintings: some were subsequently presented to important patrons. This development coincided with a new taste for collecting works on paper in the Italian peninsula and beyond. Indeed, one of the Raphael Cartoons, *The Conversion of Saul*, immediately found its way back to Italy as it was recorded in the important collection of Cardinal Grimani (1461–1523) in Venice as early as 1521.[30] It is therefore likely that all were intended to enter prestigious collections, or to be returned to the commissioner (Leo X), so that he could keep control of their reproduction or employ them as gifts; he could also, if necessary, hang them as substitutes for the finished tapestries, as was the practice in some northern European churches. The premature death of Raphael in April 1520, followed by that of the Pope in December 1521, prevented such a restitution. Instead the Cartoons remained in Brussels for an unknown period of time. The surviving seven of them re-appeared in Genoa only in the early seventeenth century.

Such highly finished cartoons came to be described in the second half of the sixteenth century as *ben finito cartone*, a new category of works that blurred the boundary between preparatory designs and works of art in their own right.[31] In order to preserve such prestigious works, praised by Vasari and his followers as the highest achievement of the graphic process and, in the case of Michelangelo's cartoon for the *Battle of Cascina*, as a real 'school for artists' (*diventato uno studio di artefici*), duplicates were produced.[32] Graphic evidence attests that the Raphael Cartoons were never used directly on the loom, as they would have been destroyed in the process.[33] Instead, copies were made. The three fragments of *Christ's Charge to Peter*, now in the Musée Condé (Chantilly, France), are probably all that is left of one of these full-scale substitute cartoons (23, 24, 25).[34] They bear a watermark identifying the paper as early sixteenth-century Netherlandish, which suggests that the Raphael Cartoons were duplicated as soon as they were delivered to Brussels.[35] This was done following a traditional method of transfer: close observation of the Cartoons reveals thousands of pin holes outlining every single detail of the compositions, from the figures and decorative elements to the architectural forms (26). These holes imply that a blank cartoon was placed under the original and they were pierced as one by a pointed tool or needle, so that the prick marks created a map of dots on the secondary cartoon. These were then joined up to create the copy.[36] At the same time, the Cartoons were cut into 90-centimetre-wide strips for easier handling and probably stored in large crates for safekeeping. This would explain their extraordinary state of preservation, despite the production of several further sets of tapestries.

This impressive collaborative work resulted in a series of ten tapestries of which seven were delivered and displayed in the Sistine Chapel on 26 December 1519; the other three had been delivered by December 1521.

›› **23, 24, 25**
After Raphael
Three fragments of *Christ's
Charge to Peter*, early 16th century

Pen and brown ink, black and red chalk,
bodycolour on paper, 39 x 50.6 cm,
57 x 75 cm and 62 x 76 cm respectively
Musée Condé, Chantilly:
PE 40 A, PE 40B and PE 40C

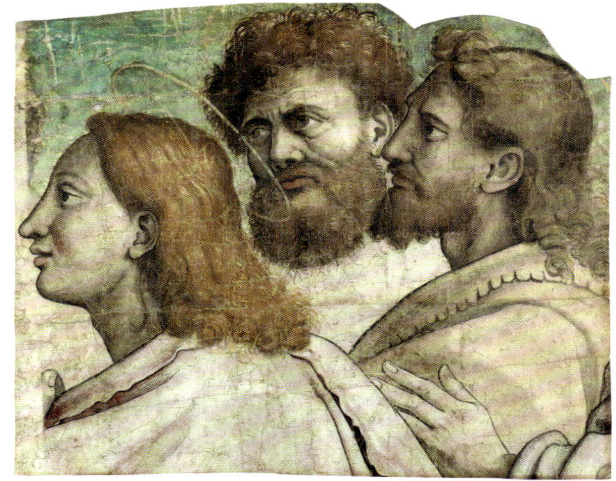

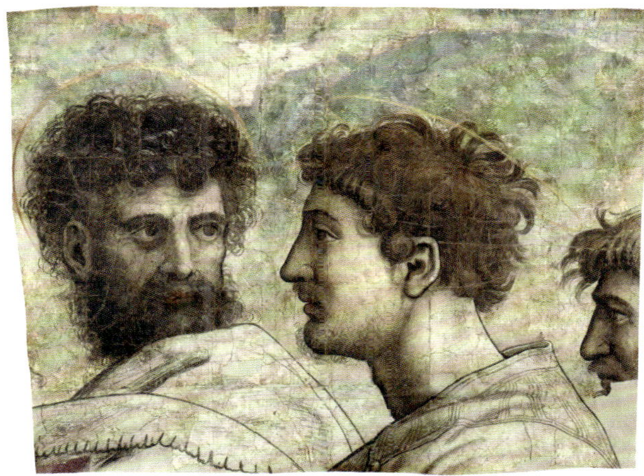

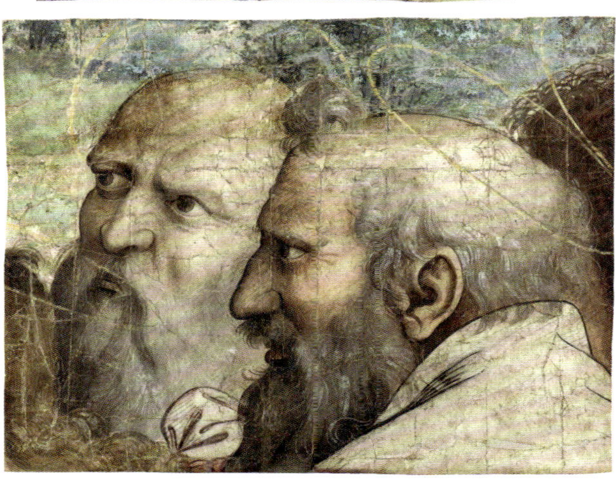

43

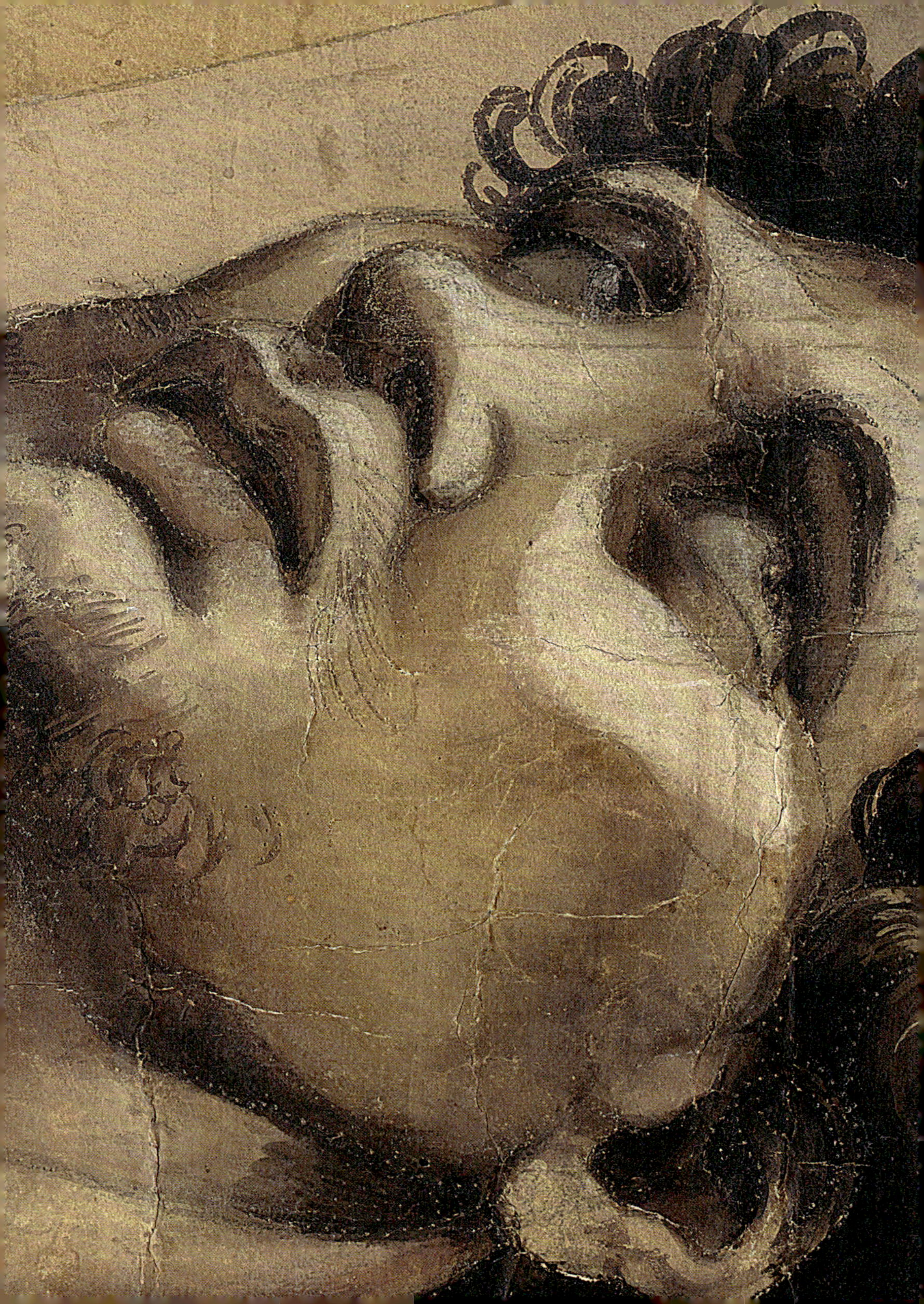

They were immediately recognized as an extraordinary achievement. The Venetian connoisseur Marcantonio Michiel (1484–1552) noted in his diary the astonishment they provoked and described them as the finest accomplishment of their time.[37] Paris de Grassis (c.1470–1528), master of ceremonies of the papal chapel, remarked that

everybody agreed there was 'nothing more beautiful in the world' (*Qui ut fuit universale judicium sunt res, qua non est aliquid in orbe nunc pulchrius*).[38]

Given the date of December 1519, it is probable that Raphael saw the tapestries in situ. Vasari himself, who saw the tapestries after they had been looted during the Sack of Rome (1527) and returned in pieces in the 1540s and 1550s (with the definitive loss of some of the borders), wrote:

> This work is so marvellously executed that it excites the wonder of those who see it that such things as hair and beards and delicate flesh-colouring can be woven work. It is certainly a miracle rather than a production of human art, containing as it does, water, animals, buildings, all so well done that they seem the work of the brush and not of the loom.[39]

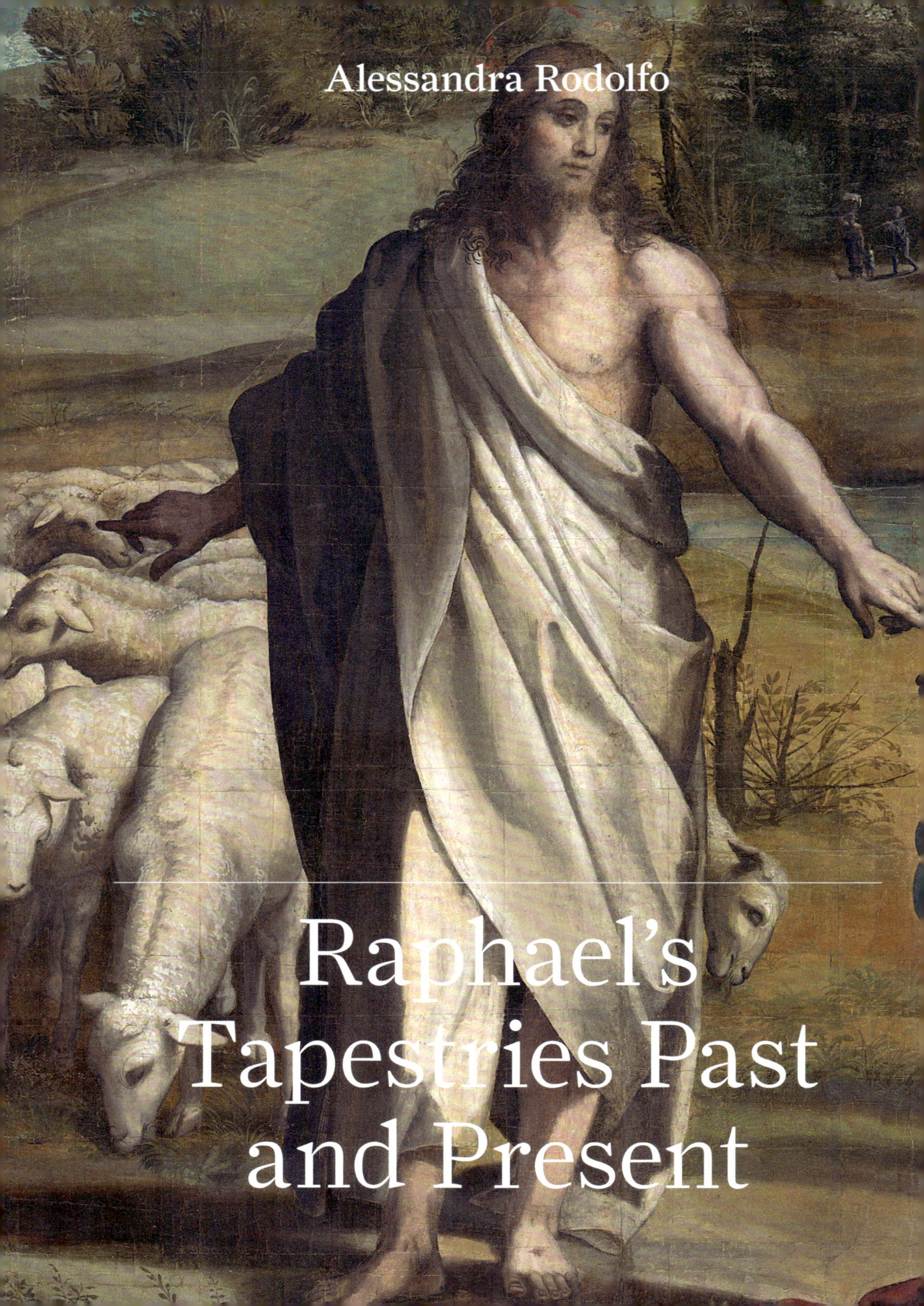

Alessandra Rodolfo
Raphael's Tapestries Past and Present

In 1517 Cardinal Luigi d'Aragona (1474–1519) was travelling through Europe together with his secretary Antonio de Beatis. On reaching Brussels they visited the workshop of the leading merchant-weaver Pieter van Aelst, who was in charge of creating the tapestries after Raphael's Cartoons. The Cartoons must have been sent from Rome in or just after December 1516 for De Beatis noted in his travel diary, *Diario di Viaggio*, that work was already underway on the tapestries, 'according to what they say, for the Chapel of Sixtus which is in the Apostolic Palace of Rome, mostly in silk and gold'.[1]

Despite the importance of the commission and extensive historical and artistic studies on the subject, there is little documentation regarding the creation of these priceless hangings. Some documents tracked down by the architect and historian Alessio Caporali in the Bini Smaghi Bellarmini Archive and recently published may add elements of interest.[2] They consist of accounts,[3] discovered in the records of the bank of Bernardo Bini, a powerful Florentine banker active in Rome in the first half of the sixteenth century, who was particularly close to Pope Leo X and under whom he held the offices of Depository of the Fabbrica di San Pietro and personal Treasurer. In addition to managing state contracts, the Bini bank met the Pope's major financial needs by advancing large sums of money, often guaranteed by the papal treasury.

Examination of documents from the Archive for the years 1518–21 clearly reveals the Bini family's contribution to Leo X's political programme, and in particular to the Pope's artistic commissions.[4] The bookkeeping records contain various accounts dated 1518, which may relate to the Acts of the Apostles tapestry set. One was made out to Cristoforo, mule driver, for the carriage of five 'bales of tapestries as in the month of June', and another to 'Pietro Leroi, Fleming, on account of tapestry-making as in the month of June 1,025 ducats',[5] which suggests a previous payment of the same amount. In January of the same year, payment of 2,000 ducats was made to 'Pietro Vanager, tapestry-maker, towards the total of 7,000 ducats on account of tapestries'.[6] In total, between 1517 and 1518, Bini paid the two tapestry-makers a total sum of 9,050 gold ducats of the Chamber (that is, ducats from the papal mint), which may have been part of the payment for the tapestries destined for the Sistine Chapel.

By December 1519, seven 'new most beautiful and precious'[7] tapestries had arrived in Rome and on 26 December of that year, St Stephen's Day, they were exhibited, as the Master of Ceremonies Paris de Grassis recalls, on the occasion of Mass in the Sistine Chapel to general amazement: 'all the chapel was astounded at the sight of them' (*tota cappella stupefacta est in aspectu illorum*).[8]

The chronicler and connoisseur Marcantonio Michiel, with exceptional 'judgement' and 'acute awareness',[9] records the display of seven tapestries during the Christmas festivities:

'considered the most beautiful thing to have been made of its kind in our day'.

The design of these hangings, according to Michiel, was undertaken by Raffaello da Urbino, for which he was paid 100 ducats for each one while their execution in fabric would have cost 1,600 ducats apiece, 'although it was adjudged and declared to amount to 20,000 ducats'.[10] This seems to be the last mention of the tapestries during the reign of Leo X, with the possible exception of a letter from the papal nuncio Francesco Chiericati – written from Rome – to Isabella d'Este, Marchioness of Mantua and patron of the arts, on 18 November 1520.[11] This speaks of a solemn mass in the Chapel bedecked with the richest hangings from the Sacristy and from St Peter's, and which art historian John Shearman tentatively links to Raphael's tapestries. By 1521 the last three tapestries must have arrived in Rome.[12]

There are contentions among scholars with regard to the number of tapestries that were commissioned – 16, as reported by De Beatis, or only 10, the existing ones[13] – and their original positioning on the walls. Shearman's seminal study[14] is based on a careful examination of the narrative woven in textile form and of how it relates to the decoration of the chapel, the liturgical ceremonies and the dimensions of the hangings. Starting from the altar wall he located the Stories of St Peter below the Stories of Christ (*in cornu Epistola*e or 'on the epistle side', that is, the north wall) with the Stories of

Display of the tapestries of the Acts of the Apostles in the Sistine Chapel in 1983

Vatican Palace, Rome; north wall with Stories of St Peter

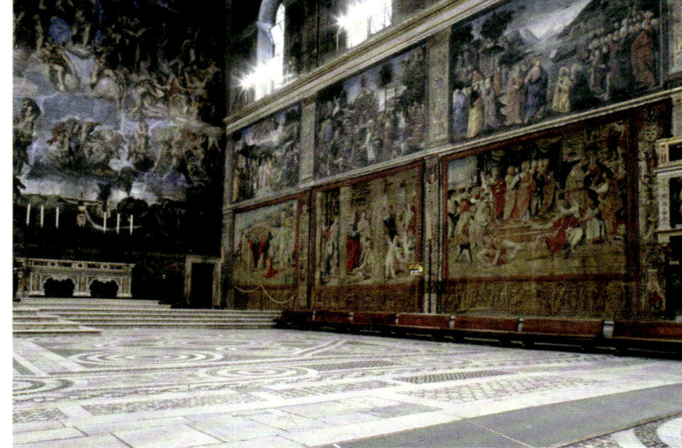

Display of the tapestries of the Acts of the Apostles in the Sistine Chapel in 1983

Vatican Palace, Rome; south wall with Stories of St Paul

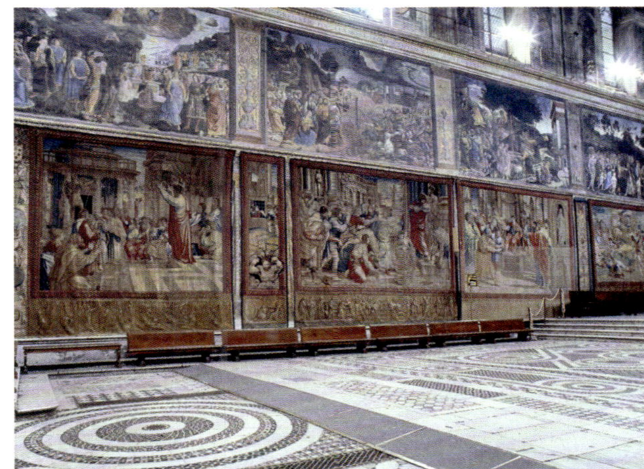

Display of the tapestries of the Acts of the Apostles in the Sistine Chapel in 2010

Vatican Palace, Rome; north wall with Stories of St Paul

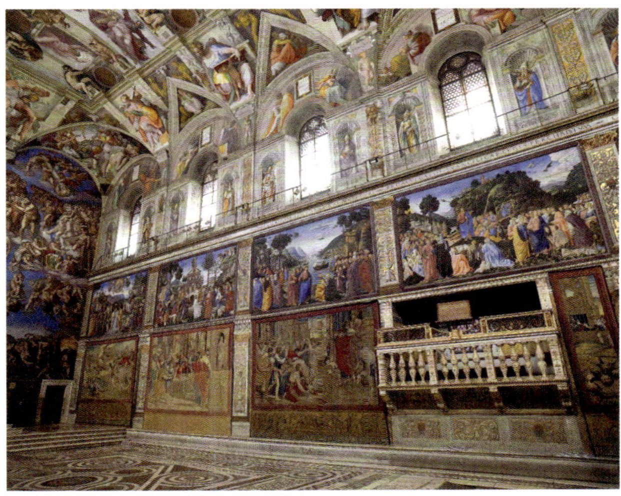

St Paul underneath the Stories of Moses (*in cornu Evangelii* or 'on the gospel side', that is the south wall) (**27, 28**). Among the most recent hypotheses, and unlike Shearman's proposal of 1983,[15] art historians Anna Maria De Strobel and Arnold Nesselrath suggested moving the Petrine cycle under the Stories of Moses (south side) and the Pauline cycle under the Stories of Christ (north side) (**29**).[16] Their proposal was based on dating the relocation of the screen (*transenna*)[17] to a period before the arrival of the tapestries, and the resulting possible placement of the only tapestry of markedly different dimensions from the others – that of the narrow *Paul in Prison* – in the limited space between the choir and the screen, where it fits well. This consideration inevitably entailed arranging the Stories of St Paul on the same side, on the north wall below the Stories of Christ, and the Stories of St Peter on the opposite wall below the Stories of Moses. This new arrangement is also supported by the fact that it places the two Apostles, Peter and Paul, representatives of the two components of the Church (respectively *ex circumcisione* and *ex gentibus*), in their traditional location: Peter being associated with the Old Testament and Paul with the New, in line with the liturgical prescriptions of Paris de Grassis.

De Strobel and Nesselrath have since produced further arguments in support of their in-depth study, strengthening their thesis with new findings. They point out that the story told in the tapestry *Paul in Prison* (according to Holy Scriptures, an earthquake struck when Paul and Silus were in prison, singing hymns to the jailers) fits with a location close to the choir, a '*tableau vivant* representing the chorus of hymns raised immediately before the tremor of the land in the account in the *Acts of the Apostles*'.[18] The two scholars also propose a new arrangement for the tapestries on the south wall. Beginning near the altar, they place the tapestry of *The Stoning of Stephen* first, then the papal throne with its reredos, followed by *The Miraculous Draught of Fishes* and the other hangings from the Petrine cycle. 'The papal throne, furthermore, would be located as though "inserted" into the stories of Peter, first vicar of Christ, making the pope a living element of the narrative.'[19] Another interesting argument is their reconstruction of the papal Mass in the Sistine Chapel on St Stephen's Day, 1519, in which they propose that the

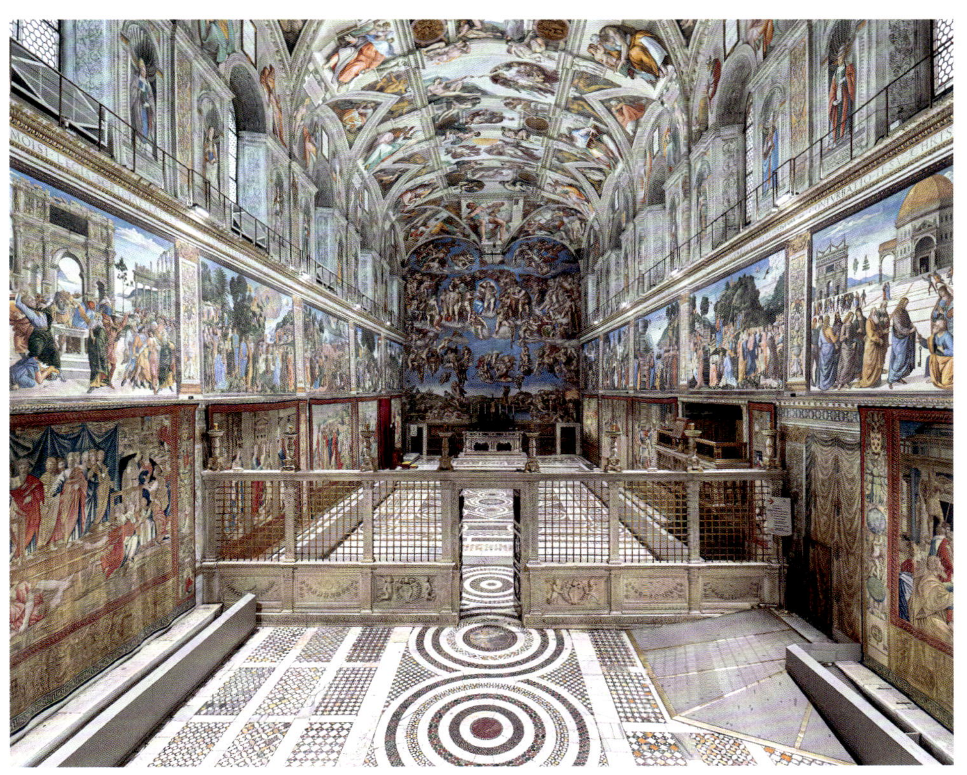

tapestry of *The Stoning of Stephen* was placed so as
to serve as an altarpiece.[20] In support of their new
hypothesis concerning the arrangement of the tapestries,
De Strobel and Nesselrath offer numerous findings as
to how the tapestries and borders should be read,
in addition to an in-depth study of the architectural
variations that took place in the chapel, and an overall
reading of the artistic and eventful history of the sacred
space and the hangings themselves.

On the occasion of the 2020 celebrations
marking the fifth centenary of Raphael's death,
the Vatican Museums wished to commemorate
the great artist with the grand 'return of the
tapestries' to the Sistine Chapel.

This was a project undertaken under the direction of the author of this chapter. It was not only intended as a tribute to the 'divine' Raphael but also as an evocative re-enactment of the ancient custom of decking the papal Chapel with precious hangings and tapestries, in memory of the solemn ceremonies of the past and of the major liturgical traditions of Christianity. Bearing in mind the need to accommodate the decorative and structural changes in the Chapel over the centuries, an evocative yet non-philological reconstruction was chosen for this purpose. All the tapestries of the Acts of the Apostles series, preserved in the Vatican collections, were displayed (**30, 31, 32**). Michelangelo's monumental fresco, *The Last Judgement*, rendered it impossible to place *The Stoning of Stephen* and *The Miraculous Draught of Fishes* on the altar wall where they were probably originally located, so these were instead hung on the south wall on either side of the throne, in the location suggested by De Strobel and Nesselrath as being the original setting.[21]

The ensemble is magnificent, displaying the decorative project of Leo X and Raphael in all its glory. The spectator's eye is drawn irresistibly down to the tapestries which, with their monumental figures and red borders, immediately attract attention to the walls, even before our contemplation of Michelangelo's ceiling, with which the tapestries seem to establish a close dialogue of compositional and stylistic references. Our intention was not only to provide visitors with a display of unique and absolute beauty but also to prompt discussions between scholars, following the round table organized in August 2019 at the V&A. This gathering had taken place on the occasion of a special viewing of Raphael Cartoons temporarily unframed.

An international group of scholars was similarly invited to see the display of the tapestries in the Sistine Chapel in order to reflect on this new proposal. The exchange of ideas was very constructive and lively among scholars who had been engaged with the subject for years, especially when it came to the question of the number of tapestries originally commissioned, their arrangement in the Sistine Chapel and the potential dialogue between the tapestries and the fifteenth-century frescoes depicted above. This new display has in fact revealed a number of inconsistencies, resulting in the

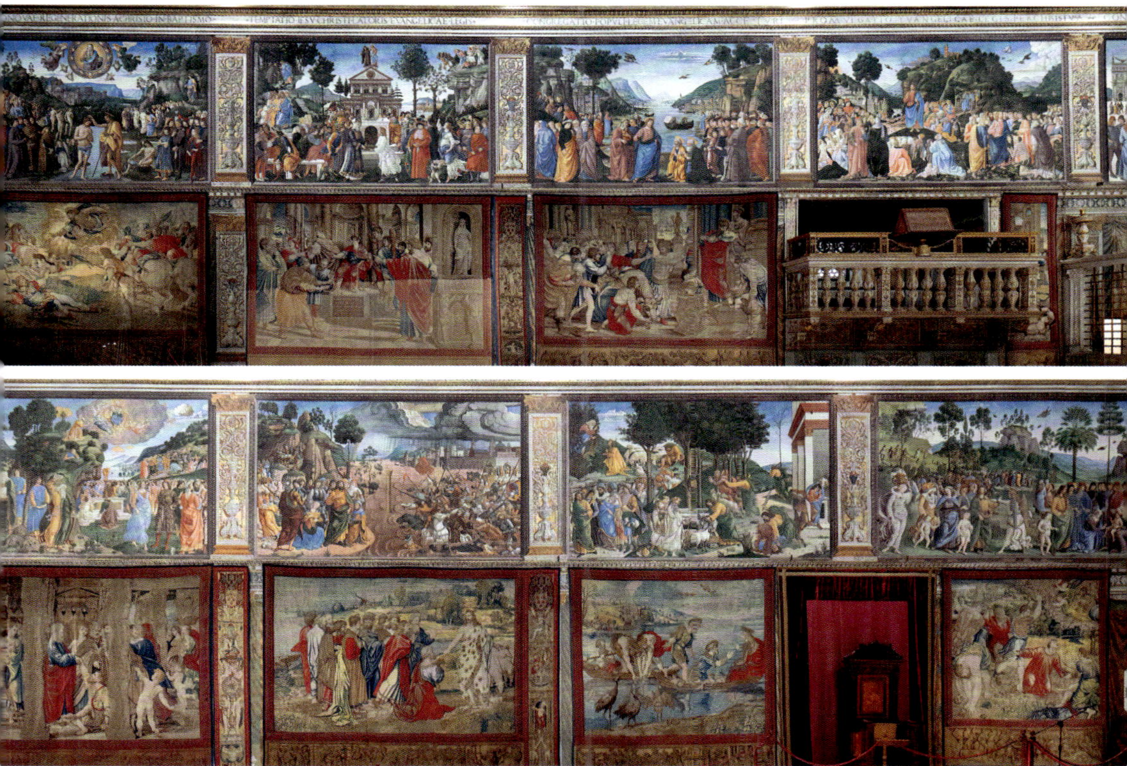

Display of the tapestries of
the Acts of the Apostles in the
Sistine Chapel in 2020

Vatican Palace, Rome; north wall with
Stories of St Paul

Display of the tapestries of
the Acts of the Apostles in the
Sistine Chapel in 2020

Vatican Palace, Rome; south wall with
Stories of St Peter

perplexing conclusion that there seems to be no definitive answer to the historical, structural and theological context of this commission: we still do not know how many tapestries were originally commissioned, when the screen (*transenna*) was moved and which theological and conceptual approach led to the display of tapestries of the saints on specific walls in relation to the Stories of Christ and Moses depicted above, the place of the papal throne and the ceremonial rules.

After the death of Leo X, during the short period when the Holy See was vacant (1 December 1521– 9 January 1522), Cardinal Francesco Armellini de' Medici (1470–1528) was acting as Camerlengo of the Holy Roman Church, an office of the papal household whose responsibilities included administration of papal property and fiscal matters. The Cardinal evaded certain payments[22] and in order to forestall the financial crisis of the Apostolic Chamber, pledges were handed over on 17 December 1521 as surety for 5,000 ducats to a Giovanni

Becher[23] (or 'Belsser', that is to say the German banker
Johann Welser) in the form of seven Raphael tapestries.[24]
Kept in the Floreria (the papal 'wardrobe') in the Vatican,
they were in effect put up as collateral in order to pay
part of the huge debts accumulated by the Pope's funeral
and the costs of the papal conclave. Two other tapestries
in the series were probably put up as collateral in the sum
of 2,000 ducats and given as a pledge to the heirs of
banker and patron Agostino Chigi,[25] who kept them for
a number of years.

At the same time, Cardinal Armellini assigned the
management of the late Pope's arrears to the company
of Piero and Giovanni Bini, Bernardo's sons and associates,
and as a guarantee of the agreements previously entered
into he delivered a substantial amount of the papal
treasury to Bernardo.

The situation appeared disastrous to the Renaissance
courtier and author Baldassare Castiglione (1478–1529),
who expressed his shock in a letter to Federico Gonzaga,
Duke of Mantua, on 16 December 1521.[26] In it he
bemoaned the fact that after Pope Leo X's death
everything had been pledged – jewellery, the 'beautiful'
tapestries, silver, the mitres and the papal tiaras,
including a precious example belonging to Julius II, which
was studded with diamonds worth 90,000 gold ducats.[27]

The tapestries must have been redeemed shortly
afterwards by Pope Hadrian VI (*r.*1522–3) and some or
all of them must have been recovered by September
1523, when they were once more displayed in the Sistine
Chapel[28] to mark the anniversary of the coronation of the
new pope. The precious hangings were again stored for
a short time in the papal Floreria, where they are recorded
in the inventory of 1524. But a few years later, during
the Sack of Rome by the Colonna (1526) and the following
year by the German Landsknechte mercenaries who put
the city to fire and sword, some of them (*The Conversion
of Saul*, *Paul Preaching at Athens* and *The Conversion of
the Proconsul*) were seized from the Pope once more,
eventually to return between 1544 and 1554.

Meanwhile, on 12 May 1527 the body of Charles de
Bourbon (1490–1527), commander of the Imperial armies
who had been killed during the Sack of Rome by the
Landsknechte, was placed in the Sistine Chapel. Adorned
with 'those rich and most beautiful tapestries of Our
Lord',[29] tentatively identified with the Acts of the

Apostles series, the Venetian historian Marin Sanudo (1466–1536) relates that he lay in state amid candles and psalms.[30] Be that as it may, according to Shearman, who suggested the presence of two of the tapestries on the altar wall, this was probably the last time the tapestries could have hung in their original position. Subsequently looted and then scattered, three of them were only returned between 1544 and 1554, by which time Michelangelo had already painted *The Last Judgement* on that altar wall (completed in 1541).

The Conversion of Saul and *Paul Preaching at Athens* shared a common fate.[31] Both were recorded in Venice, where Marcantonio Michiel saw them in the Palazzo Venier; they were then sold to the diplomat Cesare Fregoso, who took them to France, whence they returned to Rome thanks to the Constable of France, Anne de Montmorency, who had the tapestries restored as they had been badly damaged and then donated them to Pope Julius III (*r.*1550–55) in 1554. A fragment of *The Conversion of the Proconsul* was traced to a bishop of Naples, who donated it to Pope Paul III (*r.*1534–49) in 1544.[32]

What happened to the other tapestries remains unclear. Some curious and possibly tall stories appear in the writings of the Neapolitan scholar Camillo Tutini (1594–1667), who recorded in 1644 how Don Ugo de Moncada entered Rome with the Imperial army in the infamous year of 1527:

> He was the first, with his soldiery, who approached the Apostolic Palace, kicking the door of that venerable place so that it opened, to take away whatever was in it, as they did [...]. There were a number of tapestry hangings in the Sanctuary of that sacred basilica, loosely woven, with the story of the Lives of the Apostles, designed by Rafaele d'Urbino; and these they looted also. Apprised of this fact, Francis I, king of France [...] was moved to pity and gave Moncada to understand that he should sell him those tapestries. His response was to make a gift of them to His Majesty: the king of France did not accept this gift but had an estimation made of those hangings and they amounted to fifty thousand escudos, which he sent to Moncada and had the hangings sent back to St Peter's.[33]

In reality Moncada does not appear to have been in Rome
in 1527, but the news could refer to the previous year
when Ascanio and Vespasiano Colonna entered Rome
at dawn and sacked it. It is not clear, however, whether
Moncada, who was with them, participated in the
looting Tutini described.[34]

The account of the intervention of Francis I (1494–
1547) is nonetheless of considerable interest, although
unfortunately not documented in any way,[35] bearing in
mind the fact that his known desire to own a replica of
the Acts of the Apostles series dates from this very period.

Since their return to Rome around the mid-sixteenth
century, the tapestries must have been used very little
in the Sistine Chapel and there is in fact scant mention
of their presence there. They may have been displayed on
the occasion of the Mass of St Stephen in 1577, according
to the testimony of Ferdinando I de' Medici (1549–1609),[36]
who could have seen them in situ on the following
morning of 27 December that year. During the
seventeenth and eighteenth centuries, however, the
tapestries were more likely stored in the papal Floreria,
where they are recorded in the inventories, and displayed
in places such as the atrium of the Basilica of St Peter for
important events, such as papal coronations (including
those of Innocent XIII in 1721, Benedict XIV in 1740 and
Pius VI in 1775), the Opening or Closing of the Holy Door
(1724 and 1775) and the ceremonies held for beatifications
and canonizations.[37] On the occasion of the canonization
ceremonies, conducted in St Peter's, for the Spanish saint
Pedro de Alcántara and the Florentine saint Maddalena
dei Pazzi, promoted with great pomp by Spain and
Tuscany in April 1669,

'the portico of the church was decorated with
the tapestries of the Floreria Apostolica, and a
hundred and a thousand mouths were opened
in praise of that famous Raffael di Urbino who
designed them'.[38]

A painting by Giovanni Paolo Panini (1691–1765)[39] depicts
the ceremonial Opening of the Holy Door in the presence

of Benedict XIV on 24 December 1749 (33); although difficult to make out, it would appear to show one of Raphael's tapestries, *The Healing of the Lame Man*, displayed in the atrium of the Basilica above the papal canopy.[40] It is also possible to distinguish one of the later tapestries illustrating the Life of Christ (traditionally called the Scuola Nuova), designed by Raphael's collaborators. This tapestry, depicting *The Pentecost*,

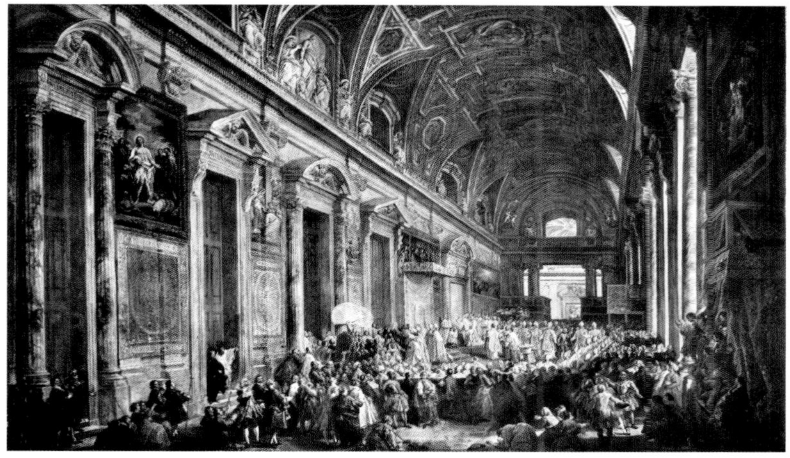

confirms early accounts of these ceremonies as displaying jointly the Acts of the Apostles series together with that of the Life of Christ (Scuola Nuova), both associated with Raphael.

> The Papal Throne stood on the right hand of the Holy Door [...] all adorned with white brocade and gold lace, the remainder of said Portico was richly decorated with crimson damask equally adorned with gold lace, mixed with Raphael's tapestries, the largest of which covered almost all the said bronze Door of the aforementioned Basilica.[41]

A watercolour preserved in the Albertina, Vienna (inv. 17463) and an engraving by Giovanni Ottaviano after Giovan Paolo Panini's son Francesco (34) record the display of the Acts of the Apostles tapestries on the walls of the Scala Regia, the regal staircase, for the Feast of Corpus Christi. A solemn and spectacular procession

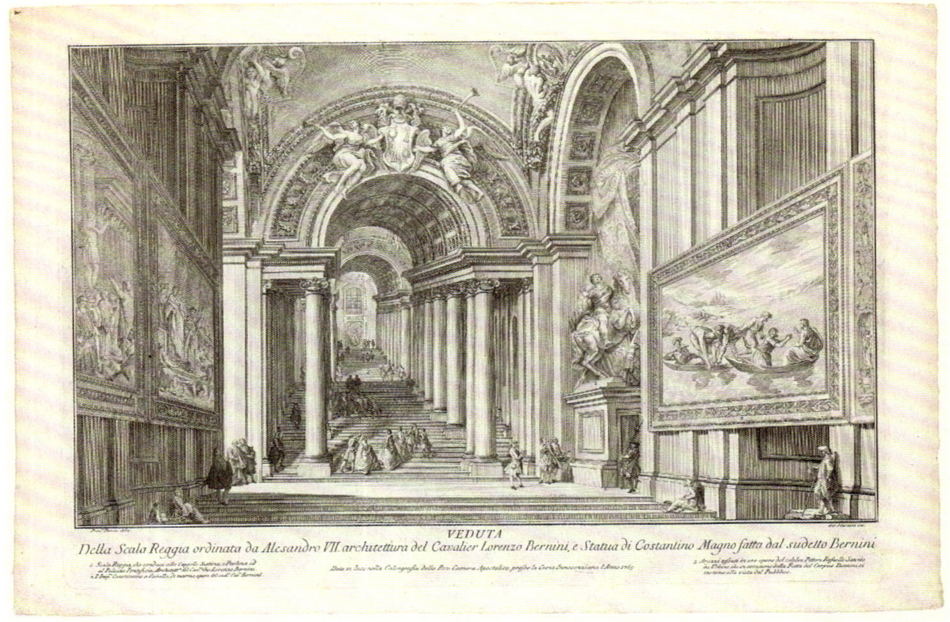

would set out from the Sistine Chapel and proceed by way
of the Sala (or regal room) and the Scala Regia, through
the colonnade of St Peter's, and part of the Borgo Vecchio
to reach the other side of the colonnade from which
it entered the Basilica. 'All this stretch of vestibules,
the colonnades and the street' were 'adorned with
magnificence and ecclesiastical pomp', according to a
contemporary written account.[42] The procession was
accompanied by a rich decorative display;[43] awnings were
placed all along the route to protect the participants from
the sun or bad weather, and the large beams supporting
them were covered with the tapestries and arms of the
pope and cardinals, painted and decorated with myrtle.
The windows of the loggias of grand buildings located
along the route were decorated with red damask. The Scala
Regia, its antechamber and the gallery beyond, however,
formed the highlight, adorned with some of the most
priceless tapestries of the papal collections, among them
those designed by Raphael and another after Leonardo da
Vinci's *Last Supper*, to honour the passage of the pope and
the Blessed Sacrament, followed by the entire Roman
Curia, to the acclaim of onlookers of every social class.

On special occasions the Raphael tapestries were most likely also displayed inside the Basilica. In the records of the Fabbrica di San Pietro, Simona Turriziani, curator of the Fabbrica archives, recently noted a previously unknown use of these tapestries.[44] During the Holy Week of 1791, the visit of the Bourbon king Ferdinand IV of Naples, and his wife, Maria Carolina of Austria, to Pope Pius VI (r.1775–99) was celebrated with great pomp. The Fabbrica di San Pietro organized the illumination of the facade, cupola and colonnade as well as the Piazza of San Pietro with a great number of torches. Inside the Basilica, the Gregorian chapel was richly adorned with damasks, velvets and 24 tapestries. Among the latter were eight tapestries borrowed from the Floreria Apostolica, described as 'large and noble by Raphael' (missing were probably *The Conversion of the Proconsul* because fragmentary, and the narrow *Paul in Prison*); the tapestries were lifted up through the windows of the high cupola where they were hung with twine and nails.

On 8 June 1787 Goethe (1749–1832), one of the pre-eminent figures in German literature, was in Rome. He had interrupted his stay in Naples, not 'without sorrow', to attend the festival and described how the tapestries displayed for the occasion had transformed 'the colonnades and open spaces into sumptuous halls and superb corridors'. The immense spaces were covered with Raphael's famous tapestries and by 'others, probably by the hands of his pupils, or contemporaries, or fellow-artists, and not unworthy of being next to the former'.[45]

After a period of some two centuries of calm, the priceless tapestries were stolen once again during the invasion of French troops under Napoleon I (1769–1821) in 1798. They were displayed in September 1801 at the Gobelins Manufactory in Paris. On comparison with the Gobelins' holdings the then director Charles-Axel Guillaumot (1730–1807) praised the papal tapestries for their design and composition but noted that they were 'totally deprived of colours and harmony' (*absolument dénuées de coloris et d'harmonie*). In 1808 they were traced by Cardinal Consalvi (1757–1824), Secretary of State to Pius VII (r.1800–23), and these tapestries including the Life of Christ (Scuola Nuova) were then bought by the papal government for 23,500 escudos from a merchant from Livorno.[46]

Restored between 1812 and 1815 at the San Michele Manufactory in Rome under the direction of Nicola Pericoli, the tapestries – previously stored rolled-up – were placed in the apartments of the 'Librarian attached to the [Vatican] Museum' and kept covered by curtains to protect them from the light. In a letter dating from 1815, Monsignor Mazzone underlined the attention paid by Pope Pius VII to these artefacts and to their new accommodation:

> Our Lord found this contrivance to be ingenious and praiseworthy, and has deigned to give you his approval; and the public, who especially on Thursday and Good Friday flocked to the Museum, which was kept open, in common accord applauded a measure carried out with such diligence, and decorum, to preserve these precious monuments of Art.[47]

The letter also expressed a series of concerns, among them doubt as to whether, for reasons of conservation, the tapestries should be displayed during the Feast of Corpus Christi – as indeed they still were in 1824, on the occasion of the opening of the Holy Door.[48]

A few years later, it was Pope Gregory XVI (*r.*1831–46) who decided to have the priceless hangings placed in the current Tapestry Gallery, once the display space of Pius VI and his ill-fated Picture Gallery. In December 1836 the *Diario di Roma* reported on the new layout and organization of the gallery, and more generally of the museums, curated by Vincenzo Camuccini, Rome's Inspector of Public Paintings, under the guidance of museums' director Antonio D'Este. It was D'Este who implemented the grandiose project, which extended from the Vatican loggias – the *Logge di Raffaello* – to the Raphael Rooms and the Tapestry Gallery, emphasizing 'a growing admiration, especially of the works of Raphael, the Vatican's greatest ornament, all bringing together the diverse glories of that Supreme Master'.[49] Just under a century later, in 1932, a new gallery opened to the public. Designed by the Milanese architect Luca Beltrami (1854–1933) at the behest of Pope Pius XI (*r.*1922–39), finally the Vatican had a permanent location in which to house its collection of paintings, culminating in the magnificent Raphael Hall (**35**).

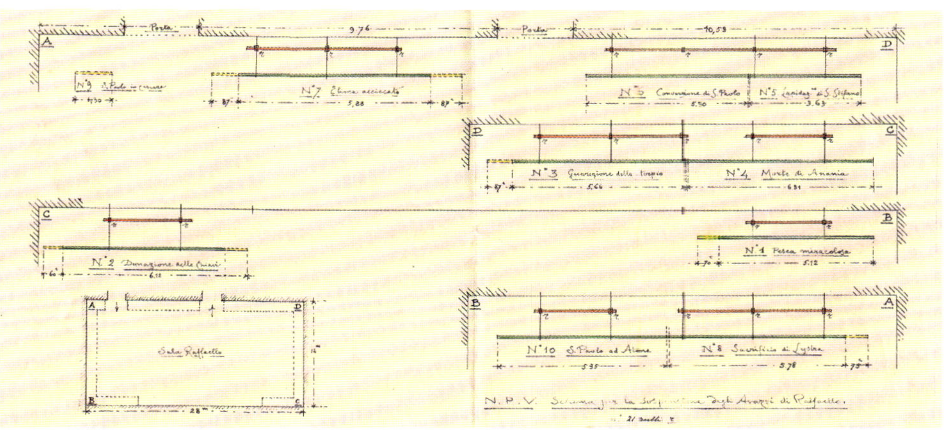

The Raphael Hall brought together three of the artist's most important pictorial masterpieces along with the series of tapestries of the Acts of the Apostles, which were placed inside specially designed display cabinets. Drawings by Beltrami show the layout of the exhibition space and the details of the display cabinets (36), together with the system devised for hanging the tapestries (37), which have been or permanent display in Room VIII of the gallery ever since. And here they remain, welcoming the twenty-first century visitor.
A new lighting system, specially designed to comply with the conservation requirements of such delicate artefacts, sets off the chromatic qualities of these priceless hangings to perfection.

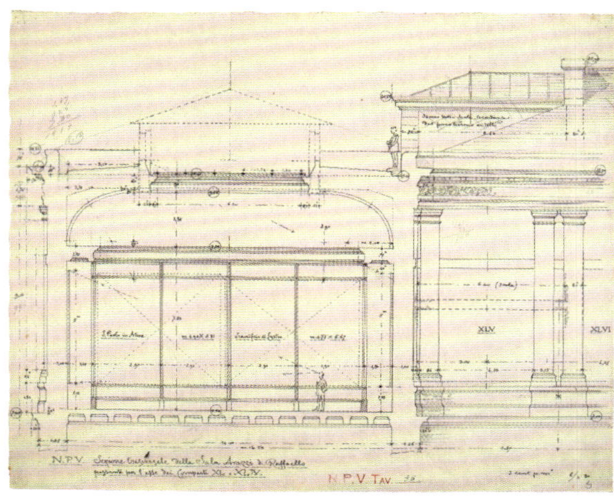

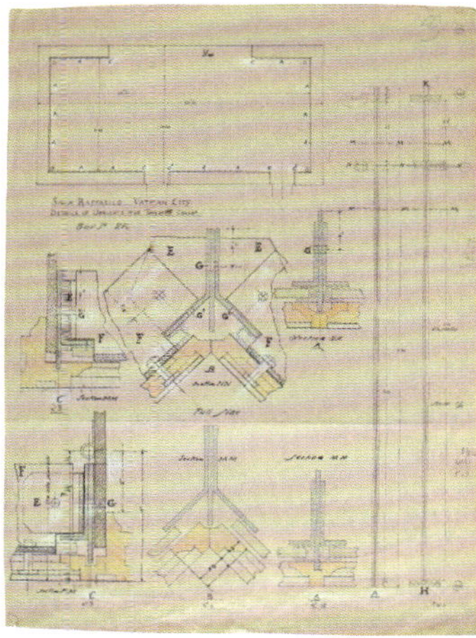

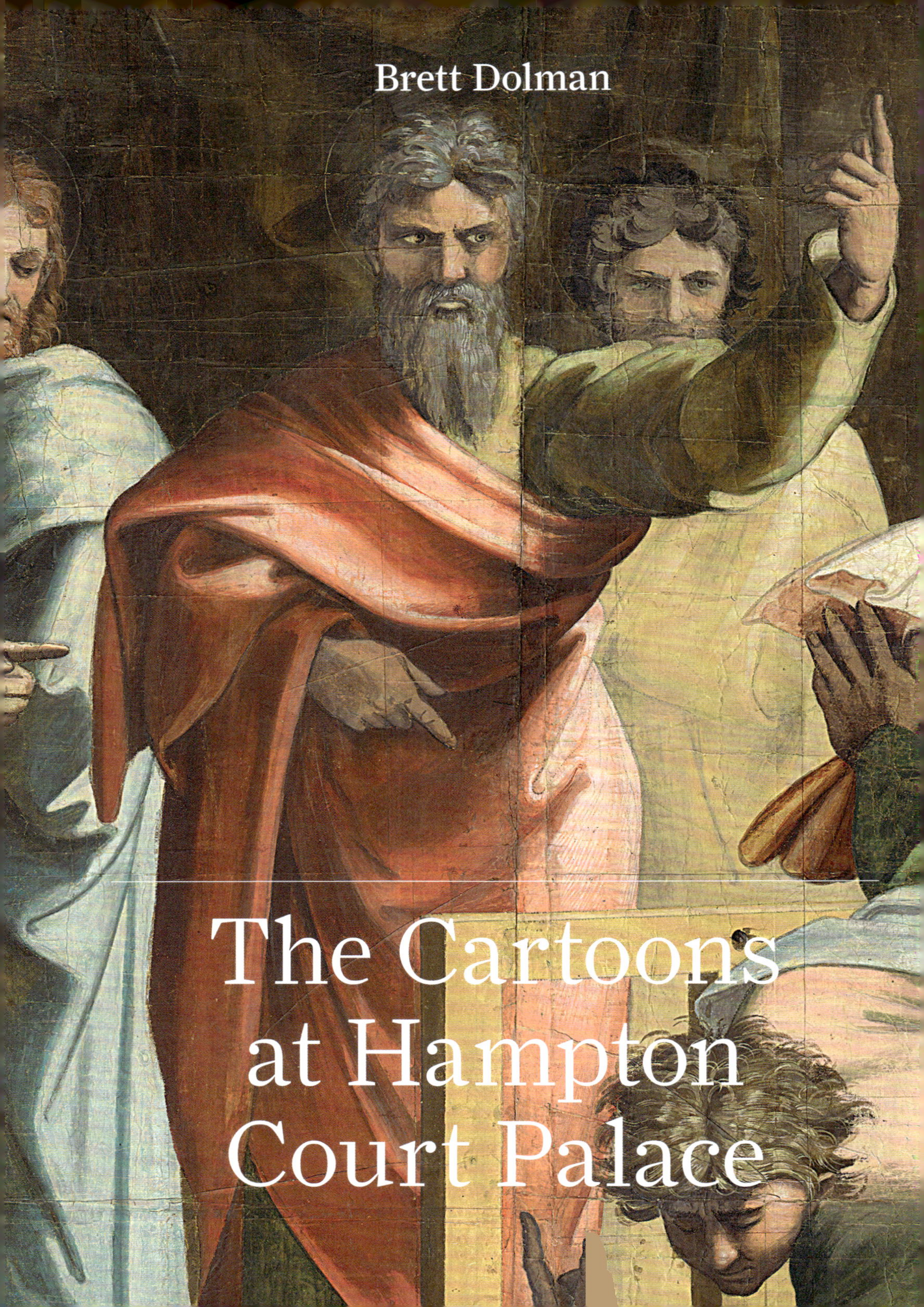

Brett Dolman
The Cartoons
at Hampton
Court Palace

In the late seventeenth century, interest in the Raphael Cartoons embraced not just their purpose in creating resplendent tapestries but also their value as magnificent and important works of art in their own right. In 1689 King William III (*r.*1688–1702) requested Philip Kinnersley, Yeoman of the Removing Wardrobe (*fl.*1675–89), the royal department charged with moving royal furniture and furnishings between palaces, to unpack the artworks from their 'large case' for inspection at the Banqueting House in Whitehall. The king's secretary and art advisor, Constantijn Huygens (*fl.*1628–97), described how the Cartoons were spread out on the floor 'and they were very fine, better than the prints made thereof by the best masters'.[1] At this stage, Raphael's designs were still divided into vertical strips, for the convenience of the tapestry weavers; this made appreciating them as artworks challenging and unsatisfactory.

To facilitate the experience, Parry Walton (*fl.*1679–99), 'mender and repairer of the King's pictures', together with John Norris (*fl.*1669–1702), Joiner of the Privy Chamber, and possibly the artist Henry Cooke (1642–1700), all became involved from 1691 in the project to conserve the Cartoons, to glue the strips together, attach them to stretchers and frame them for display at Hampton Court, where work had begun on constructing a new royal palace. Probably by 1694 the Cartoons were hanging in the incomplete King's Gallery at Hampton Court in a temporary arrangement, so that they could be viewed and copied more easily. In that year, the young Irish artist Charles Jervas (1675–1739), assistant to the King's principal painter Sir Godfrey Kneller (1646–1723), was permitted to 'make Sketches in Little after ye Cartoons'.[2] Presumably taken down soon afterwards and returned to store, the Cartoons were back on display three years later. In 1697 palace carpenters were paid for erecting scaffolds, and the smith, William Bache (*fl.*1672–97), was commissioned to provide '35 hooks and 14 loops to hang the Cartoons in the King's Gallery'. On 2 September, Charles Hatton (*c.*1635–?) wrote to his brother Christopher, Viscount Hatton (*c.*1632–1706). after a visit to the ongoing palace building works, that 'the sight best pleased me was the Cartoons by Raphael, which are far beyond all the paintings I ever saw'.[3]

William III's wife, Queen Mary I (*r.*1688–94), had also taken an interest in the display of the Cartoons, as part of the decorative programme for Hampton Court's new interiors. Her death in 1694 had been one of the reasons why building work stalled until 1699, when William III finally committed resources for their completion. The King's Gallery was redesigned specifically to create a permanent home for the Cartoons, with specially designed panelling and elaborately carved framing mouldings by Grinling Gibbons (1648–1721) and a marble chimneypiece by John Nost (d.1710). On 12 September, the Comptroller of the Royal Works, William Talman (c.1650–1719), informed the King that:

'the gallery for the Cartoones of Raphell is so forward that I shall fix up the pictures in a week'.[4]

 All seven Cartoons were hung in an elevated position, in a symmetrical arrangement designed for aesthetic impact, rather than reflecting the chronological sequence of the biblical narrative: one of the pieces was slightly enlarged to enhance the effect. Green silk curtains were installed for their protection when the room was not in use, but the new gallery was soon furnished and became the usual location for meetings of William III's Privy Council, as well as one of the first purpose-designed art galleries in Britain (38).

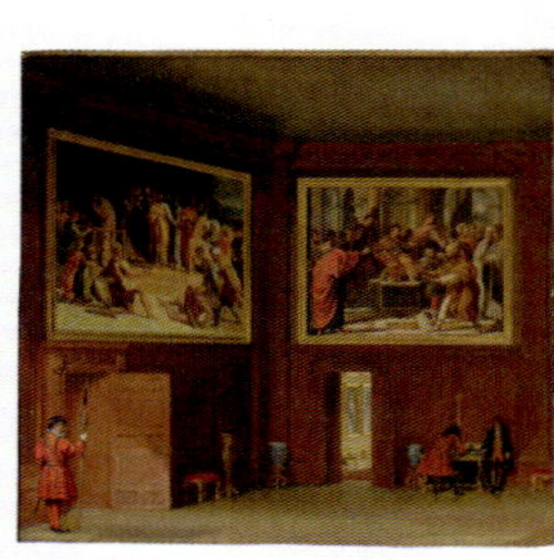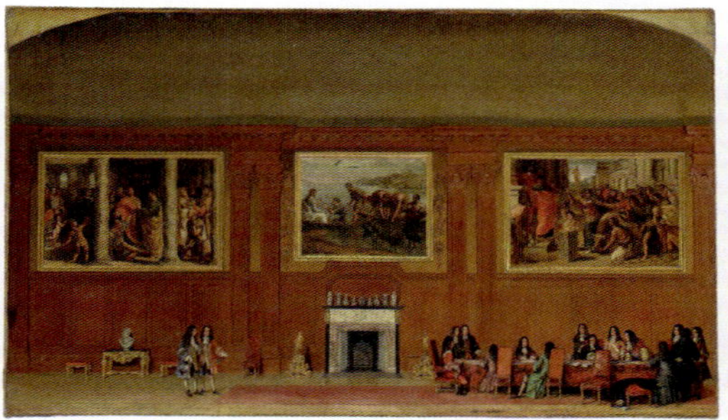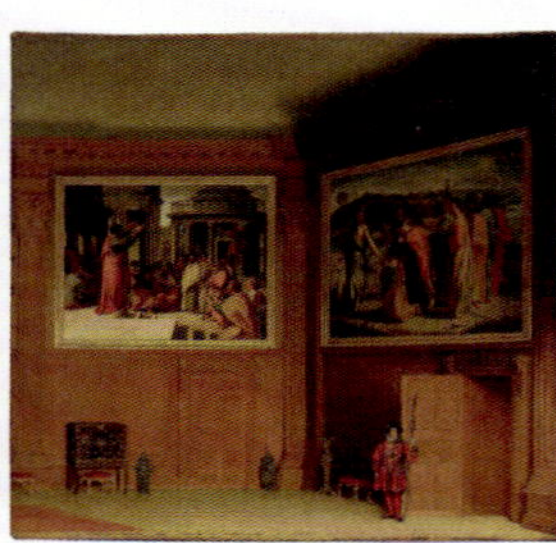

William III's 'Cartoon Gallery' stood at the heart of a set of new royal apartments at Hampton Court, with an interior decorative programme designed not only to reflect the latest 'baroque' fashions, but also to project the image of the king. William had been invited to seize the throne in 1688, deposing his uncle and father-in-law James II (*r.*1685–88); his authority, unlike the Stuart monarchy's assumption of 'divine right', now depended on a constitutional agreement with Parliament, tying the king to a new role as protector of the Anglican state. Consequently, the art that decorated the walls at Hampton Court was a mixture of dynastic portraiture, establishing William as a genuine y Stuart king with the right to be on the throne, and newly commissioned murals and sculpture asserting his credentials as a Protestant soldier and leader, pitched against the vices and corruptions of the Roman Catholic church and the expansionist policies of Louis XIV, King of France (*r.*1643–1715).[5]

Within this scheme, the Cartoons were both an aesthetic celebration of William III's high culture and a statement of his religious faith. They represented a direct connection to the New Testament, a pure and truthful vision of the Stories of St Peter and St Paul, despite the fact they had originally been commissioned by the Head of the Catholic Church, Pope Leo X. Religious tracts of the early eighteenth century frequently sought inspiration from direct quotation from the New Testament, and the Cartoons were seen as the dynamic visual expression of this sanctified primary source material. A year after William III's death in 1702, the physician and poet Richard Blackmore (1654–1729) published *A Hymn to the Light of the World*, describing the Cartoons in an illustrative appendix to his epic religious poem and making the connection between the transformative experience of Gospel truth and Raphael's awe- nspiring 'wonders'.[6]

William's ownership and display of the Cartoons emphasized what many Protestants saw as the Christian purity of the King's approach to religious policy, as he sought to embrace more dissenters within a wider definition of Anglicanism through the Act of Toleration of 1689. The establishment in 1698 of the Society for Promoting Christian Knowledge (SPCK) created a populist movement dedicated to the dissemination of Anglican Christian pamphlets, bringing the story of the New

Testament to the widest audience, while engraved prints of the Cartoons transmitted this message in visual form. After 1702, the Protestant credentials of Queen Anne (*r*.1702–14) were similarly linked to the Cartoons. As Richard Steele (*c*.1672–1729) wrote in *The Spectator*, 'the whole work is an exercise of the highest piety in the painter ... these invaluable pieces are very justly in the hands of the greatest and most pious sovereign in the world'.[7]

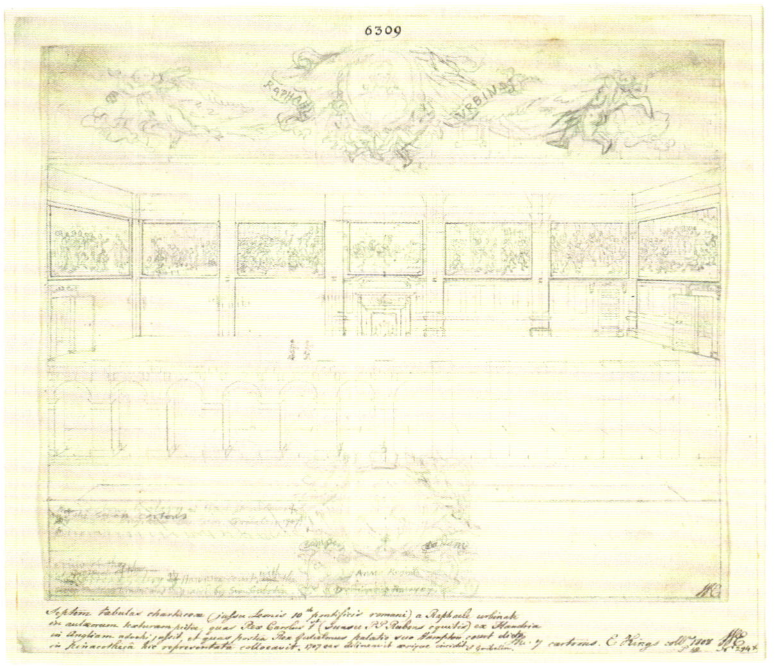

⌄ **39**

Simon Gribelin (1661–1733)
Sketch of the original hang of Raphael's Cartoons in the new King's Gallery at Hampton Court, 1707

Pencil on paper, 18 x 21 cm
Royal Collection Trust: RCIN 917314

The fame of the Cartoons, celebrated as important artworks and as visual expressions of British piety, encouraged artists and visitors to Hampton Court to view, study and copy them (**39**). Throughout the early decades of the eighteenth century, various painters received the Lord Chamberlain's permission to make copies, among them Sir James Thornhill (*c*.1675–1734) and James-Christopher LeBlon (1667–1741), while engraved prints were created by Simon Gribelin (1661–1733), Sir Nicolas Dorigny (*c*.1658–1746) and others, and widely circulated.[8]

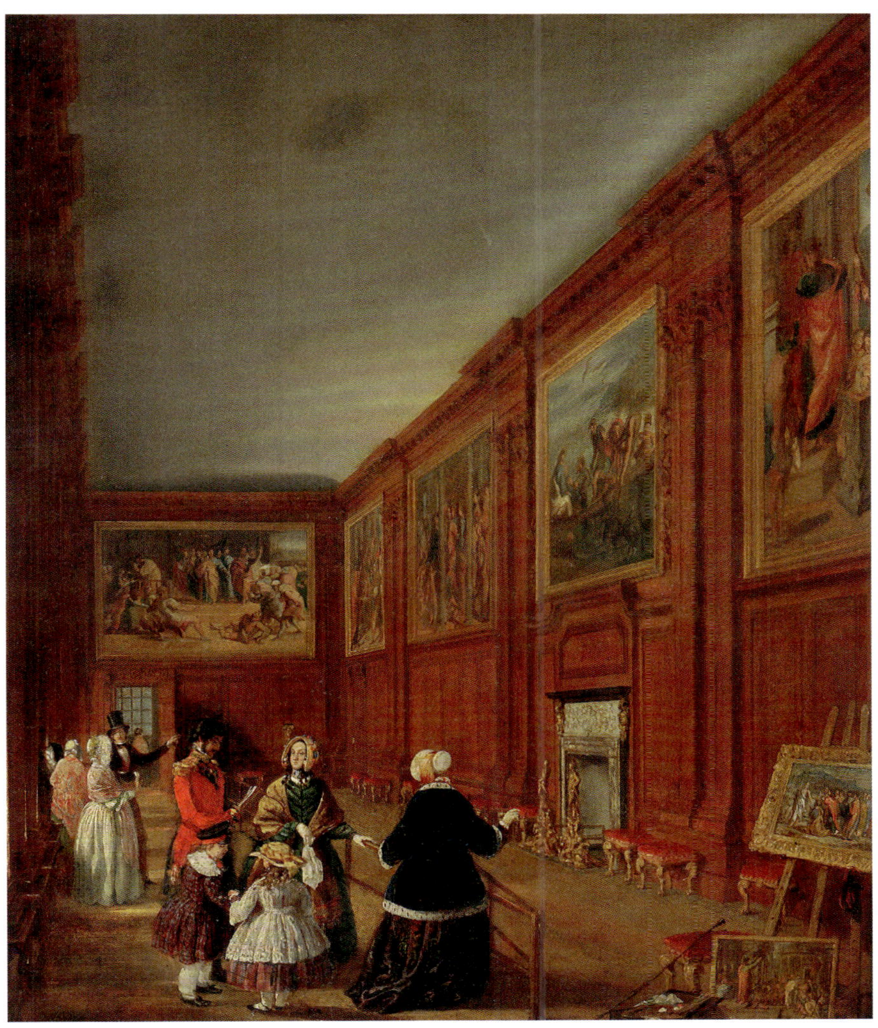

Raphael generally, and the Cartoons specifically, began to occupy a central position in British art historical treatises and academic primers.

Queen Anne and the early Hanoverian monarchs continued to use Hampton Court, but their visits became infrequent and stopped altogether after the death of Queen Caroline in 1736. Gradually the state apartments at the palace assumed a new identity as a tourist attraction, part of a domestic version of the Grand Tour for 'polite tourists' of the right social class (40). Early connoisseurial guidebooks described Hampton

Court as a palace of art, with the Cartoons the aesthetic climax to the visit; the English portrait painter and collector Jonathan Richardson (1665–1745) described the palace as that 'great School of Rafaelle'. Not all tourists were appropriately awe-struck, however, with *The Idler* satirizing their 'cant of criticism [and] that volubility which generally those orators have who annex no ideas to their words'.[9]

Despite their popularity and importance, the Cartoons were still perceived by the monarchy as its personal property, part of a royal art collection that could be moved around among palaces and re-displayed according to royal need. The acquisition of Buckingham House by King George III (*r*.1760–1820) and Queen Charlotte (1744–1818) in 1762, and its subsequent remodelling by the architect William Chambers (1722–1796), gave the new king and queen an opportunity to re-arrange their collection according to their own tastes. Stephen Slaughter (*c*.1697–1765), Surveyor of the King's Pictures, was paid for 'making out new lists and taking the dimensions of his Majesty's pictures at the palaces of Kensington, Hampton Court and Windsor Castle', while historian Horace Walpole (1717–1797) recorded how 'the King and his wife are settled for good and all at Buckingham House, and are stripping the other palaces to furnish it'. In December 1763 the Raphael Cartoons were removed from Hampton Court and re-hung in Queen Charlotte's new saloon on the first floor, in giltwood 'Carlo Maratta' frames which were then the current style, displayed around three walls over a light green damask wall hanging (41).[10]

John Boydell (1720–1804), whose new guide to the Cartoons was published in 1764, hoped that more people would be able to see them in their new home, while Richard Dalton (*fl*.1778–91), Royal Librarian and later Surveyor of the King's Pictures, argued that they would be better preserved away from 'damp' Hampton Court. But visitor access to Buckingham House proved difficult, and the visibility of the Cartoons became a topic of controversy. In 1777 the radical politician John Wilkes (1725–1797) railed against their removal to Buckingham House, calling the Cartoons 'a national treasure, a common blessing … [not] private property'.[11] Britain did not have a national collection, still less a gallery to put it in, but it did have a royal collection that some

›› **41**

A plan of the Saloon or Great Room in the Queen's Apartments, Buckingham House, *c*.1774

Pen and ink and watercolour, 54.7 x 74.8 cm
Royal Collection Trust: RCIN 926323

›› **42**

A plan of the Cartoon Gallery, Hampton Court, *c*.1804

Pen and ink and watercolour, 36.5 x 52.8 cm
Royal Collection Trust: RCIN 918068

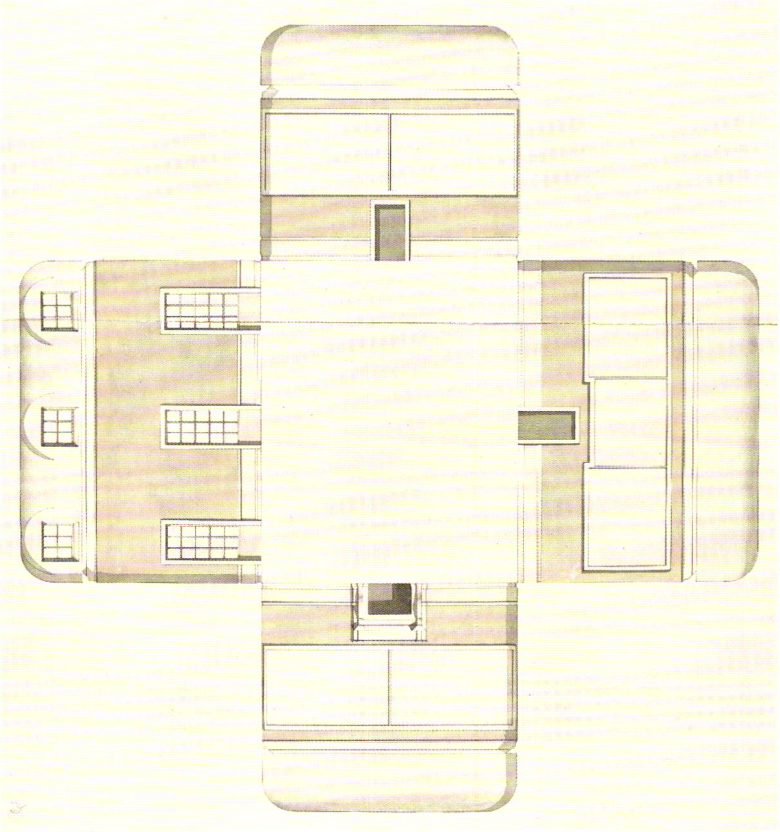

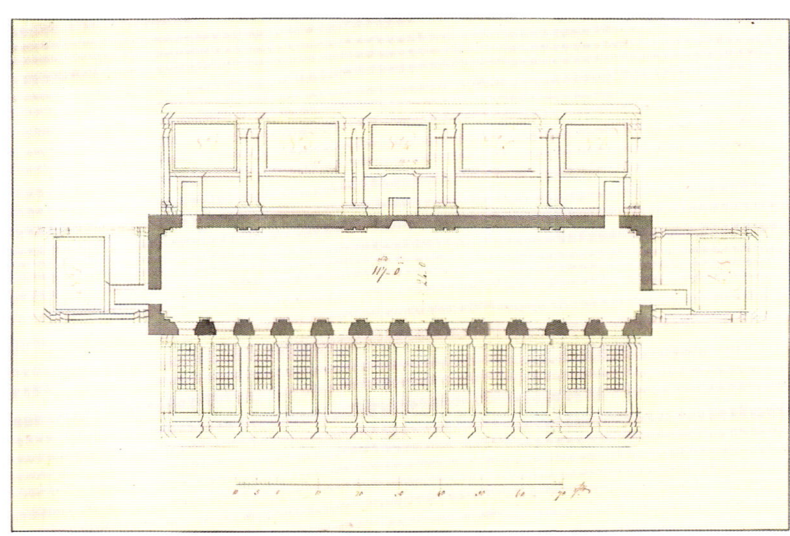

began to see as a shared national resource. There was a growing perception that this ought to be accessible to all, or at least all those educated to an appropriate degree of artistic sophistication.

In 1780 the historian Johann Jacob Volkman (1732–1803) wrote that access to Buckingham House to see the pictures was forbidden, whilst in 1783 Walpole described how he had only been able to obtain 'a slight view of the Queen's apartment'. Soon afterwards, in 1787, the Cartoons were moved to the state apartments at Windsor Castle, 'open to public inspection', as Dalton wrote in *The Gentleman's Magazine* of that year.[12] But the spatial challenges at Windsor meant that Raphael's seven Cartoons had to be separated into two groups: four in the King's Presence Chamber (*The Conversion of the Proconsul, The Death of Ananias, Christ's Charge to Peter* and *Paul Preaching at Athens*) and the remaining three in the Queen's Presence Chamber. In both rooms, interestingly but probably unintentionally, Raphael was reunited with Baroque murals by Antonio Verrio (*c.*1639–1707). Verrio had been commissioned to work at Windsor by Charles II (*r.*1660–85) but he later became one of the artists employed by William III at Hampton Court to express his iconography of Protestant supremacy.

The unsatisfactory experience of separating the Cartoons, as well as George III's plans to transform Windsor into a Gothic palace, ultimately led to their return to Hampton Court in 1804, 40 years after they had been removed (42). The decision was nonetheless partly influenced by public demand: the presence of Raphael at Hampton Court in the earlier eighteenth century had defined the art collection there as special and many still considered the palace to be their natural home. New ideas as to how the Cartoons ought to be displayed were invited, with due consideration to be given to Raphael's original scheme: the artist's alleged endpieces, *The Sacrifice at Lystra* and *The Death of Ananias*, once again bracketing the display. According to the artist and diarist Joseph Farington (1747–1821), George III was directly involved, along with the artist Benjamin West (1738–1820), Surveyor of the King's Pictures from 1791, in the decision to replace the Cartoons in 'the room intended for them by King William'.[13]

Problems of access to the Cartoons nonetheless remained; their elevated position in the Cartoon Gallery made them difficult to see, without taking them down or raising a scaffold to a convenient height, while there were continuing concerns about damp: spray from the fountain in the courtyard outside reportedly entered the gallery through open windows. To improve artists' access to the Cartoons, the Prince Regent (1762–1830) authorized their loan to the British Institution between 1816 and 1819 (two each year, followed by the seventh) while *The Conversion of the Proconsul* and *Christ's Charge to Peter* were lent to the Royal Academy in 1821 and 1822. But the constant re-hanging and moving of the Cartoons created fresh concerns that more damage would be done in the process, while West, now in his 79th year, caught a severe cold while superintending the packing of *The Death of Ananias* in 1816![14]

In the 1820s the architect John Nash (1752–1835) considered moving the Cartoons to the newly named Buckingham Palace to hang in George III's Octagon Library, which he proposed to convert into a private chapel. But this would have re-opened once more the debate about public access to the celebrated treasures of the royal collection. Indeed, by the early 1800s the visitor profile of Hampton Court had changed: well-heeled and informed tourists of the eighteenth century had been joined by a growing number of ordinary day-trippers. Farington, at the palace in 1814 to study the Cartoons with West, the engraver Thomas Holloway (1748–1827) and the artist Thomas Lawrence (1769–1830), described how 'many of the country people and from London dressed in large Sunday attire came in large parties to see the palace'.[15]

Public access to art subsequently became a subject for debate in the House of Commons.

Between 1835 and 1836, the Select Committee on Art, chaired by the progressive Liberal MP William Ewart (1798–1869), questioned a succession of arts administrators, business leaders, artists, dealers and collectors, with the aim of improving training and standards of domestic design in all forms of national artistic production. The National Gallery had been established in 1824 with a small collection of paintings purchased for the nation from the collection of John Angerstein, including the *Raising of Lazarus* by Raphael's great rival, Sebastiano del Piombo, and in the 1830s the architect William Wilkins (1778–1839) was employed to create a suitably grand new home for the collection in Trafalgar Square. The artist Benjamin Haydon (1786–1846) was not alone in hoping that the new gallery might include the Cartoons, declaring, 'Good God, can any man doubt if People saw these fine things every day in the National Gallery their taste would not be improved'. In 1836 the Select Committee concluded, 'It would be a great public benefit if the celebrated Cartoons from Hampton Court could be deposited in the National Gallery ... the pictures particularly sought for in our national collection should be those of the era of Raphael'.[16]

However, the Cartoons could not be moved without royal approval and there was a degree of concern that transferring such treasures to a public institution might challenge the jurisdiction of the Surveyor, or even their status as part of a private royal collection. William Seguier (1772–1843), in the awkward position of being both Keeper of the National Gallery and Surveyor of the King's Pictures (succeeding West in 1820), resisted the move, claiming that, 'the smoke of London in twenty years would destroy them'. Instead, despite the Committee's recommendations, the Cartoons remained in Hampton Court, where access was improved in 1838 by the abolition of entrance fees for visitors and for artists wishing to copy artworks (it had previously cost over £4 for a permit to copy the Cartoons). At the same time, hundreds of paintings not required by the royal family elsewhere were moved to Hampton Court, and the state apartments were transformed into a public picture gallery of over 600 pictures.[17]

The new public galleries at Hampton Court were not universally acclaimed. The collection was criticized for the inconsistent quality of the works on display, the lack of curatorial organization and interpretation, and the subdued lighting, particularly in the Cartoon Gallery. The Cartoons themselves were also considered at risk from the opposing threats of damp and fire, both from the stoves used to heat the state apartments and the open fires kept by the 'grace-and-favour' residents who still occupied the apartments above the galleries. Thomas

Uwins (1782–1857), Surveyor of the Queen's Pictures from 1844, drew attention to 'the decay into which they are rapidly falling', and *The Spectator* led a public campaign arguing for their removal to the National Gallery throughout the 1840s.[18]

Richard Redgrave, Uwins' successor as Surveyor from 1856, did much to professionalize the curatorial approach at Hampton Court, instituting a managed conservation regime and organizing the first official photography of the Cartoons (43). His subsequent appointment at the South Kensington Museum, together with Prince Albert's enthusiasm for Raphael, ultimately ensured that the Cartoons would move to London after all. In 1865, four years after her husband's death,

Queen Victoria gave permission for Hampton Court's greatest artistic treasure to become one of the star attractions of the South Kensington Museum, where it could be displayed in a safer, more instructive context.

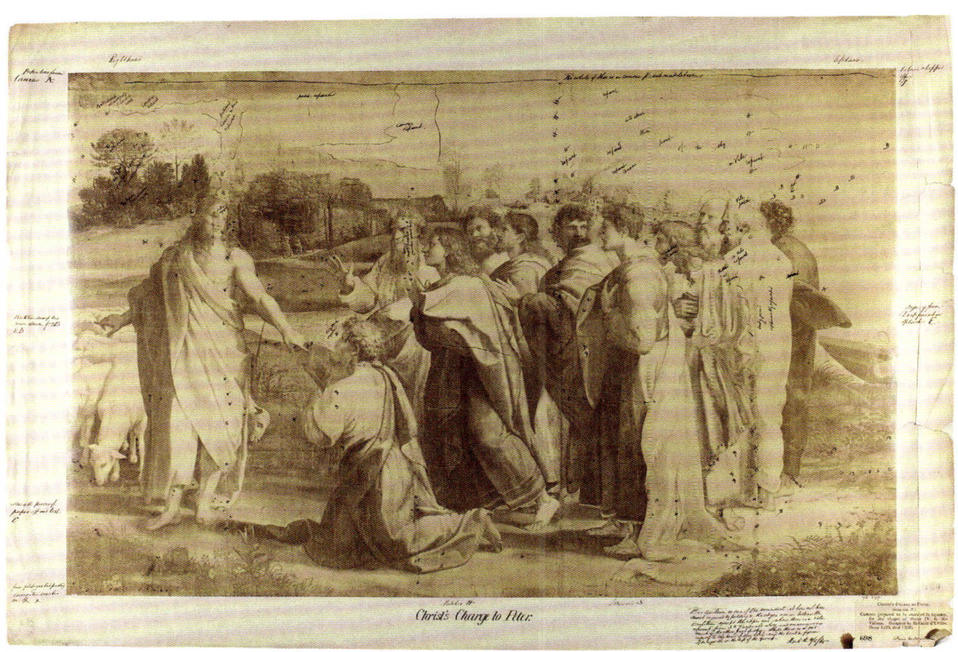

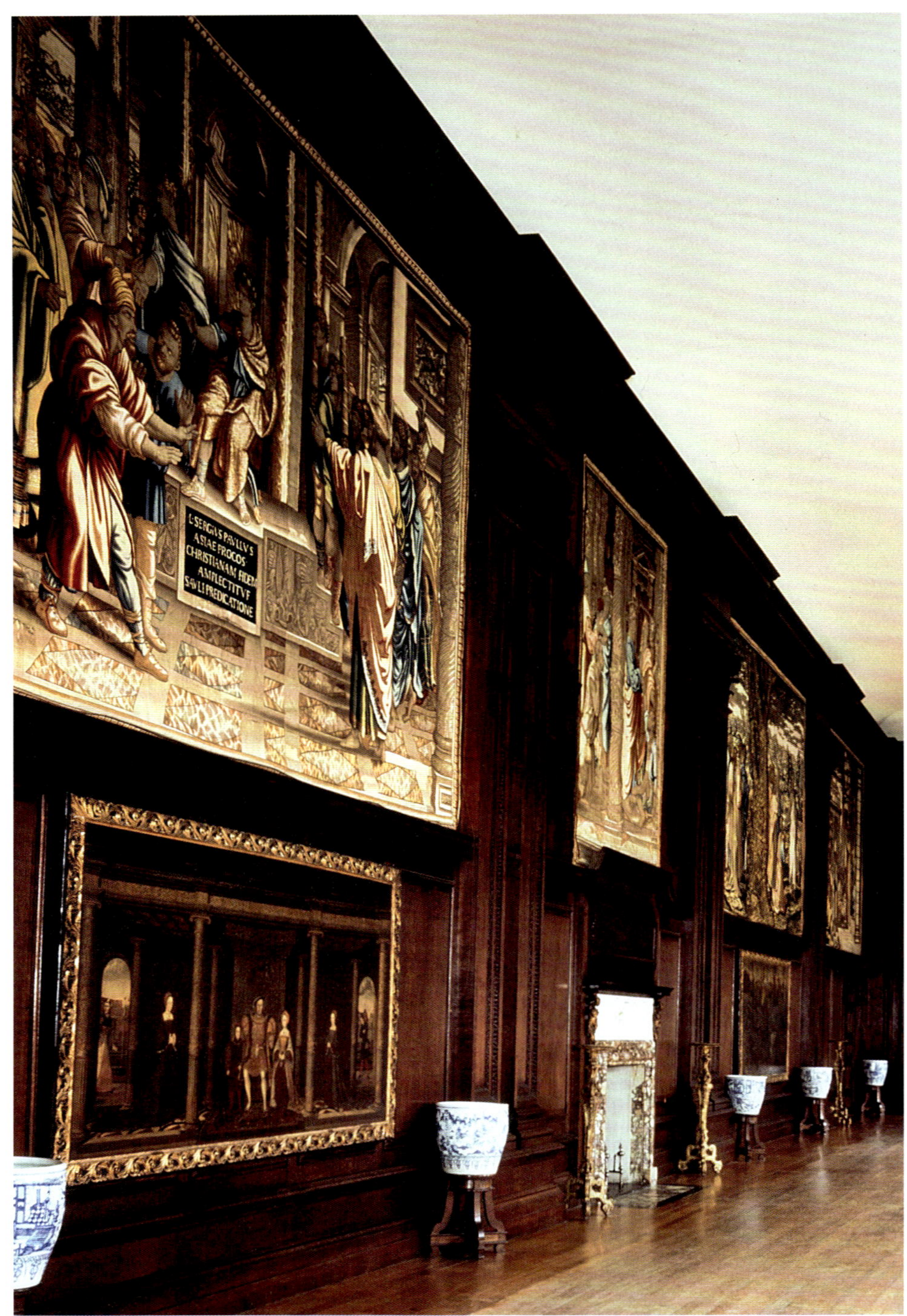

L·SERGIVS PAVLLVS
ASIAE PROCOS
CHRISTIANAM FIDEM
AMPLECTITVR
SAVLI PREDICATIONE

From 1865, different curatorial visions re-imagined William III's Cartoon Gallery at Hampton Court. Redgrave introduced partitions along its length, allowing for a dense hang of artworks in a re-christened 'South Gallery'. In the early 1900s, the partitions were replaced by a set of eighteenth-century tapestries of the Acts of the Apostles, derived from Raphael's designs, with King Edward VII (r.1901–10) insisting that if the South Kensington Museum (now the V&A) had the original Cartoons, then Hampton Court ought to have the tapestries (44). Finally, after a major fire swept through the King's Apartments in 1986, Historic Royal Palaces completed a major restoration of William III's state apartments and installed a set of full-size painted copies of the Cartoons.[19] Today, the crowded Victorian picture galleries have been dismantled, but Hampton Court remains a spectacular home for treasures of the Royal Collection, and the Cartoon Gallery acts as a reminder of its important role as a palace of art.

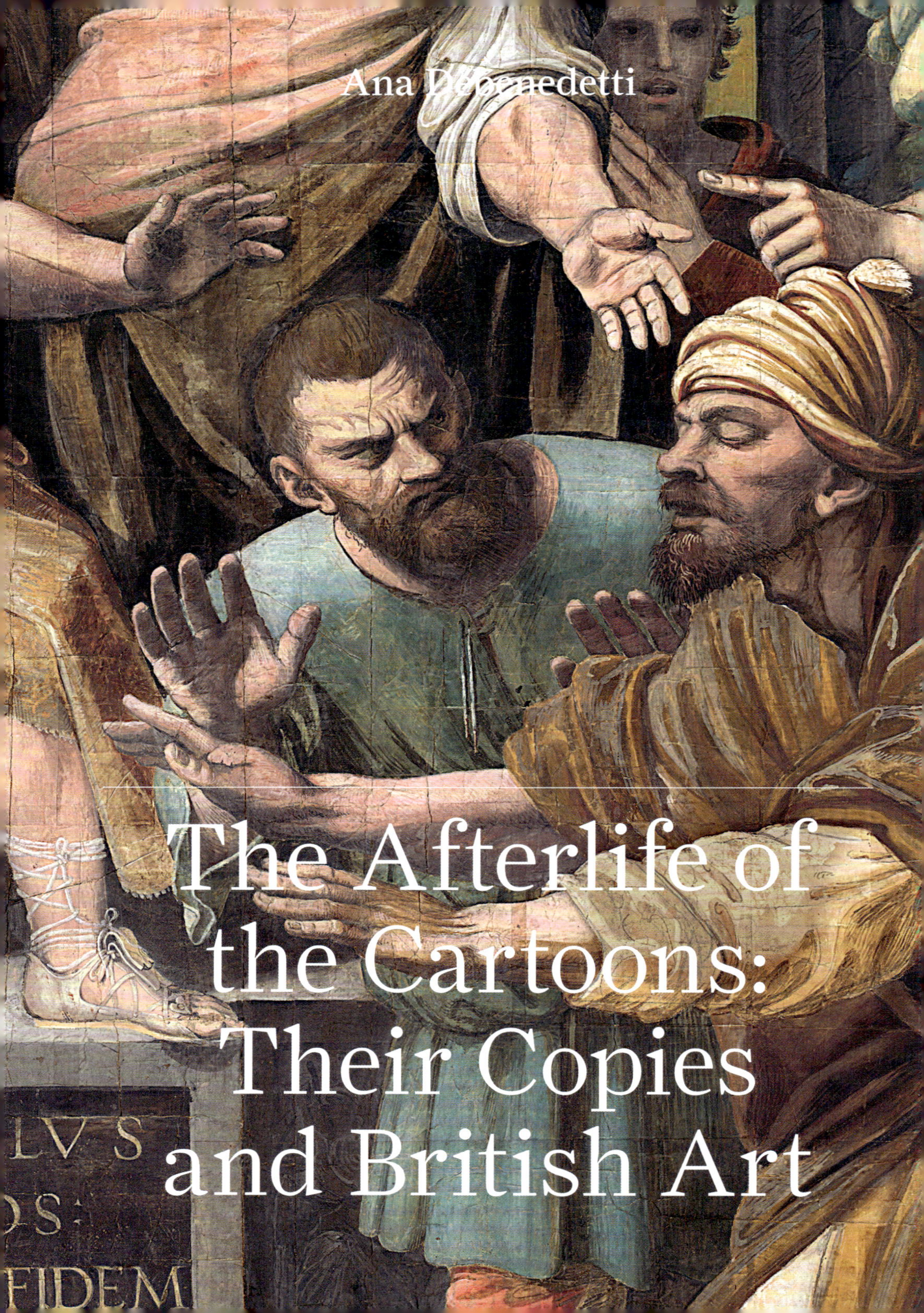
Ana Debenedetti
The Afterlife of
the Cartoons:
Their Copies
and British Art

The tapestries delivered to the Vatican between December 1519 and December 1521 were among the first of a long series of copies after Raphael's much-admired Cartoons. These, together with the mythological scenes from the *Stufetta* (Cardinal Bibbiena's bathroom), were the first of his monumental works to be engraved and published.[1] As early as 1516, by which time the Cartoons were already inaccessible having been sent to the tapestry weaving workshop in Brussels, Raphael had prints engraved after a selection of his preparatory studies by professional engravers including his regular collaborators: Marcantonio Raimondi (1480–1534), also the author of an intimate portrait of Raphael (45); Agostino Veneziano (c.1490–c.1540); Marco (Dente) da Ravenna (1493–1527) and Ugo da Carpi (c.1480–1532), who seem to have been occasional members of his workshop.[2] Vasari reports:

> Raphael, having made the cartoons for the tapestries of the Pope's chapel, later woven in silk and gold, with stories of St Peter, St Paul and St Stephen, Marcantonio engraved the preaching of St Paul, the Stoning of St Stephen and the Healing of the blind man [*sic*], prints equally beautiful, for Raphael's invention and grace of design and the finished engraving of Marcantonio which is indeed unsurpassable.[3]

Raphael, of course, did not make the engravings himself, but the close collaboration between Raphael and the engravers suggests that he might have had some influence in their making. Only four of the ten original designs seem to have been engraved in Raphael's lifetime: *The Death of Ananias* and *The Conversion of the Proconsul* of c.1515–16 by Agostino Veneziano, *Paul Preaching at Athens* of c.1517 by Marcantonio Raimondi (the others are considered copies after Veneziano's prints) and *The Miraculous Draught of Fishes* in 1518 by Ugo da Carpi. Examples of these engravings can be found in private and public collections including the V&A (46).

These prints encompass two techniques, copperplate engraving and chiaroscuro woodcut, that convey the pictorial manner of the Cartoons and also Raphael's strong sense of the distribution of figures within the picture plane. Raphael had the prints made to

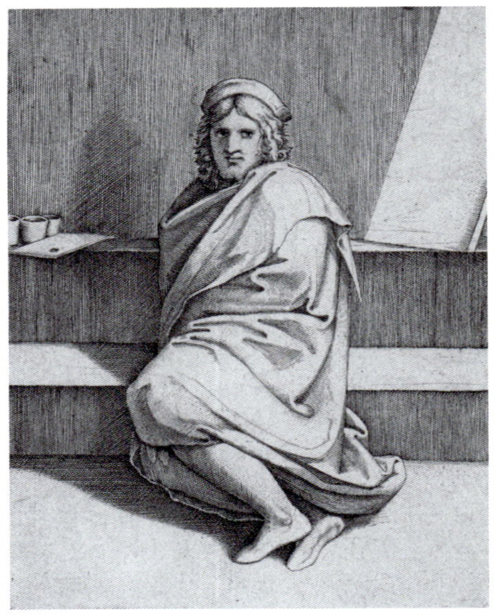

disseminate his inventions to fellow-artists and also, for commercial purposes, to a wide public. Legend has it that after his death, the proceeds of their sale were meant to go to the woman he loved (Margherita Luti, often identified with the so-called Fornarina).[4] The prints

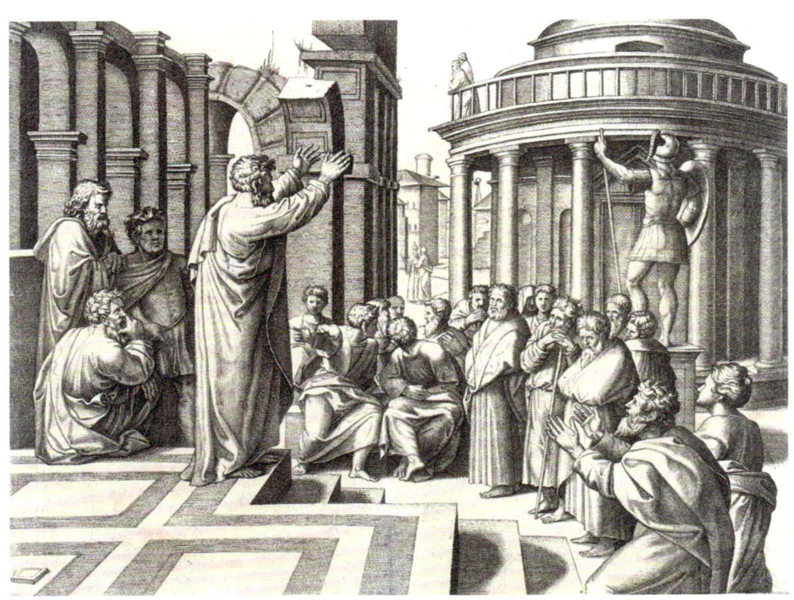

played a large part in spreading Raphael's influence among artists in Italy and beyond. As early as July 1517, Andrea del Sarto (1486–1530) had drawn upon *The Conversion of the Proconsul* for his fresco *The Arrest of the Baptist* in the Chiostro dello Scalzo in Florence.[5] A century later, the foremost exponent of Raphael's art in Rome and France, Nicolas Poussin (1594–1665), together with his fellow French academicians, continued to draw on Raphael's designs, as attested by a series of paintings.[6] His influence would hardly ever wane.

As stated by Vasari, the engravings, like the tapestries, are a translation of Raphael's designs into a different medium and can therefore be construed as re-interpretations rather than straightforward copies. The Sistine tapestries themselves do not copy exactly Raphael's designs. The weavers took the liberty of adapting some parts by adding strips of landscape or additional organic ornament to ease the reading of the woven designs. Differences can also be noted in the colours and patterns in the figures' garments, intended to avoid solid areas of plain colours, which were disliked in tapestry. The same discrepancies are found in the engravings and other objects, such as maiolica plates, Limoges platters and later plaquettes, which reproduced the printed models (**47, 48, 49**).[7]

47 (left)
Nicola Pellipario (d.1542)
Plate depicting *The Conversion of the Proconsul*, *c.*1530
Urbino

Polychrome maiolica
Civici Musei del Castello Sforzesco, Milan: 124

48 (centre)
Martial Courteys (*c.*1544–1592)
Platter depicting *The Death of Ananias*, *c.*1580
Limoges

Polychrome enamel, gold and copper with foil, 40.6 x 54.9 cm
Los Angeles County Museum: AC1992.152.117

49 (right)
Patanazzi workshop
Plate depicting *Paul Preaching at Athens*, late 16th century

Polychrome maiolica, 43 cm diam.
Pinacoteca e Musei Civici, Pesaro: 4153

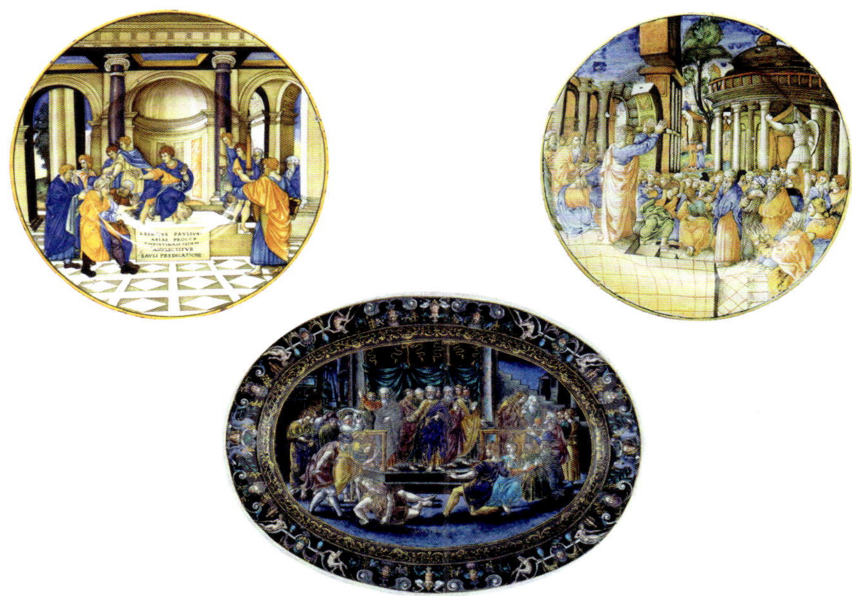

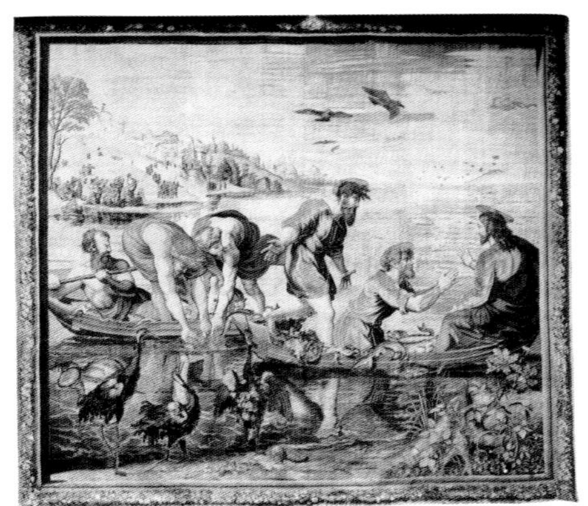

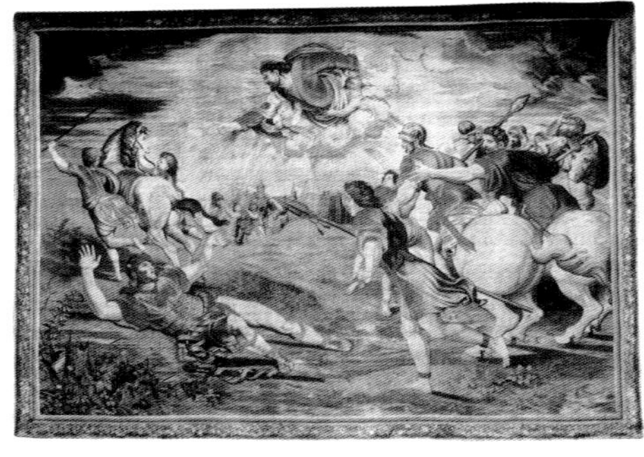

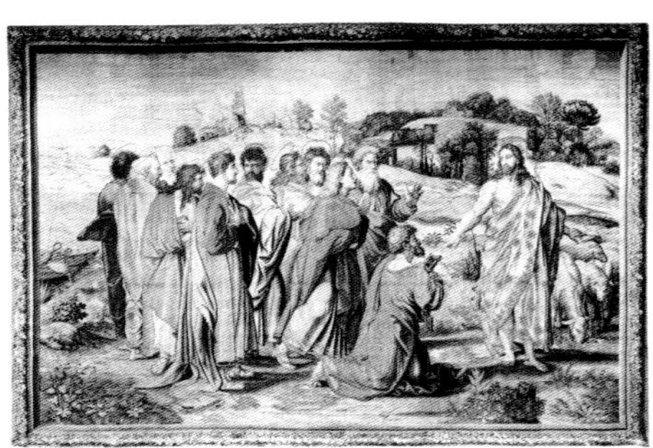

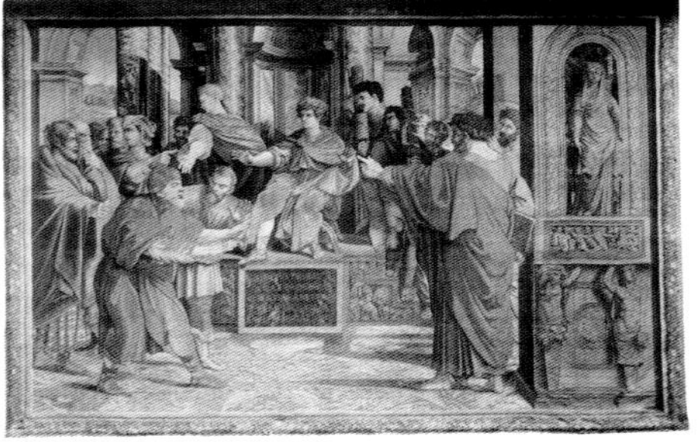

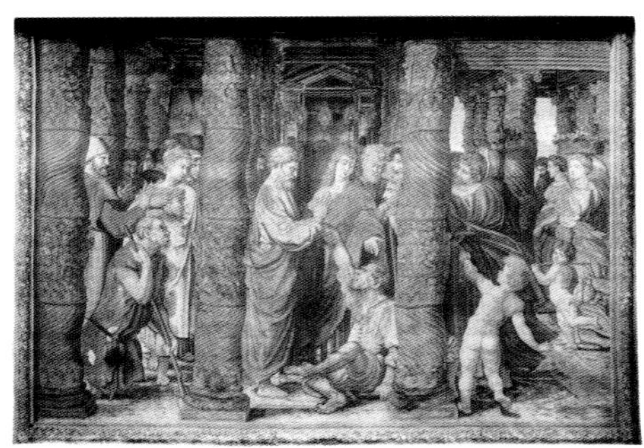

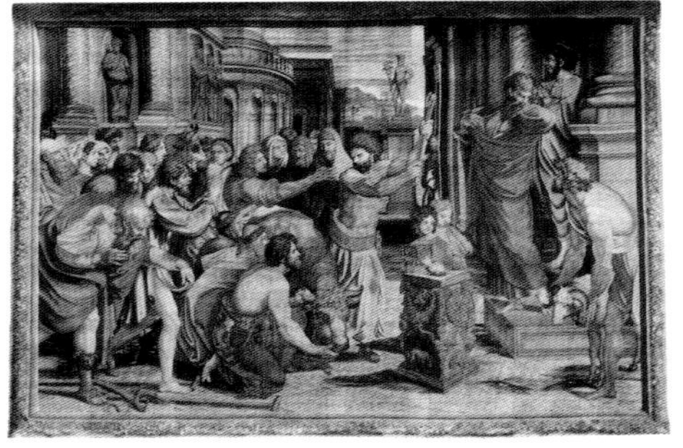

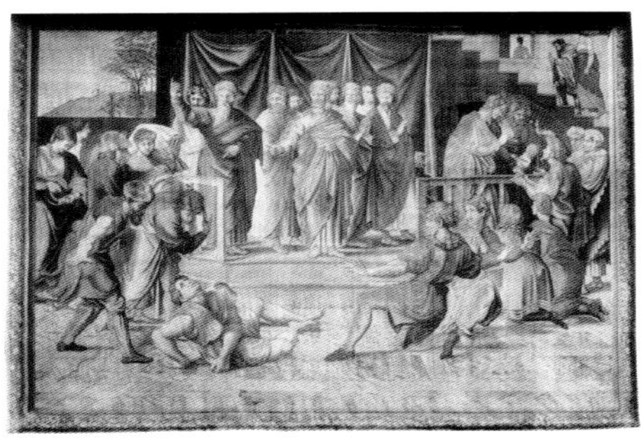

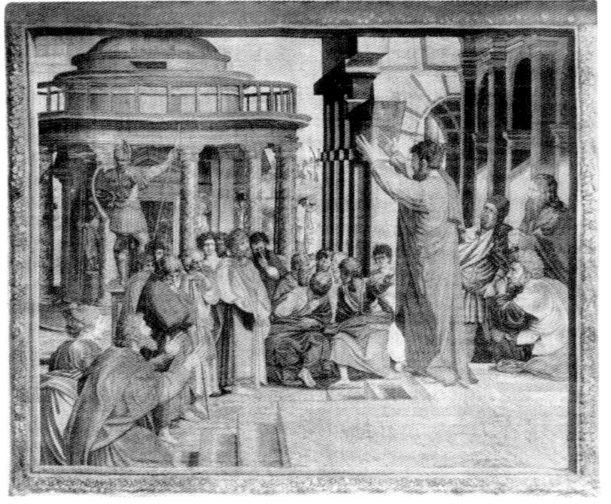

Despite the fact that the Cartoons remained lost for nearly a century, further sets of tapestries were produced throughout the sixteenth century. Full-scale duplicates of the Cartoons must have passed between different workshops in Brussels: a set for Francis I of France was woven in about 1533, followed by another for Henry VIII of England (*r.*1509–47) in 1542 (both destroyed), while a fourth was made for the Emperor Charles V (*r.*1519–56), or his son Philip II of Spain (*r.*1556–98; today in the Patrimonio Nacional, Madrid) and a fifth for Cardinal Ercole Gonzaga (1505–1563) of Mantua in the 1550s (still extant in the Palazzo Ducale, Mantua). These later sets show comparable minor design adaptations and must have had similar borders to those of Francis I's tapestries, which were distinct from Pope Leo X's set.[8]

Henry VIII's tapestries, copied from Raphael's Acts of the Apostles series apart from the borders, may be considered as the first point of contact between the art of Raphael and a British public, albeit largely restricted to the court and important visitors (**50**).[9] They were possibly commissioned for the newly refurbished Banqueting Hall in Whitehall Palace (1542) following a propaganda campaign, which placed the King as new apostle to his own people after he declared himself Supreme Head of the Church of England in 1531.[10] Being moveable goods, these tapestries were subsequently hung in various royal palaces. However, the Tudor series did not prompt further reproductions of any kind, unlike the original set on the Continent, where copies in various forms continued to be issued throughout the sixteenth and seventeenth centuries, continuously inspiring European artists.[11] They seem to have had no influence at all on painting or design in Britain.

In this context, it might at first seem surprising that in 1623 the Prince of Wales, the future Charles I, ordained for

‘certaines patterns to be brought out of Italy, and sent to us into England for the making thereby a Suite of Tapestry’.[12]

These 'patterns' were the full-scale tapestry designs now known as the Raphael Cartoons, which had recently

re-emerged in Genoa. What happened to the Cartoons
between 1516, when they were sent to Brussels, and 1623
remains a mystery. Tradition has it that it was the painter
Peter Paul Rubens (1577–1640) who drew the Prince's
attention to this hidden treasure. Rubens had seen the
Cartoons during his years in Italy, perhaps around 1600,
as graphic evidence attests.[13] Seven Cartoons were
purchased by Charles from an unknown source in
Genoa while two others are recorded in the collection
of Ferdinand II de' Medici (1610–1670) in Florence.[14]
The latter, *The Stoning of Stephen* and *The Conversion
of Saul*, together with *Paul in Prison* are still missing.[15]

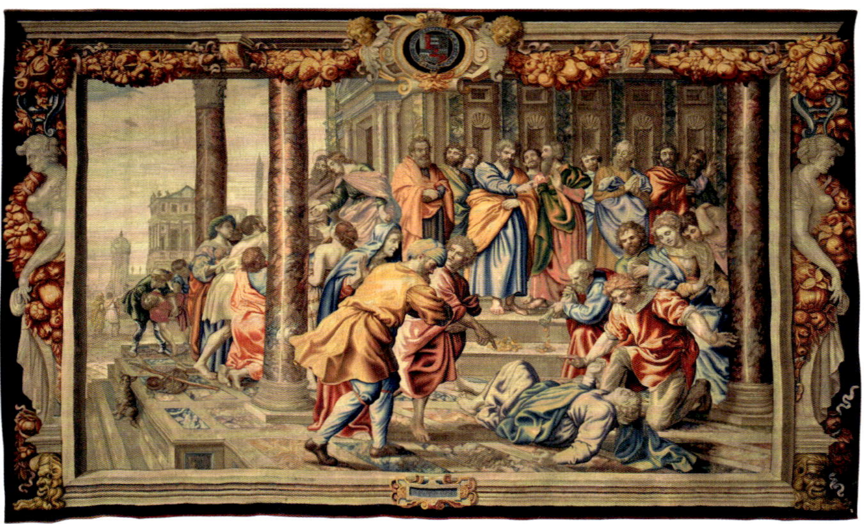

The Cartoons were acquired specifically to be used
at the tapestry manufactory established in the village
of Mortlake, west of London, in 1619. Following traditional
practice, full-size copies of the Cartoons were then made
by the German-born painter Francis Cleyn (*c*.1582–1658),
who was appointed the manufactory's official designer
under the supervision of its director, Sir Francis Crane
(*c*.1579–*c*.1636). These secondary cartoons were used
for the new weavings, while Cleyn probably copied
the missing designs from the set made for Henry VIII.
He also created a further scene, the *Death of Sapphira*,
a companion piece to Raphael's *The Death of Ananias* as
Sapphira, wife of Ananias, was also found guilty of the

Mortlake manufactory tapestry
after Raphael (1483–1520)
Sacrifice at Lystra, c.1641

Wool, silk and gilt-metal-wrapped
thread, 535 × 720 cm
Mobilier national, Paris: GMTT 16/5

sin of withholding charity. The only known surviving weaving of this later scene was part of a set made for the Earl of Pembroke, now in the collection of the Duke of Buccleuch at Boughton House, Northamptonshire (**51**).[16]

The influence of Raphael's designs was, however, short-lived in England. Further faithful woven copies were issued by Mortlake looms throughout the seventeenth century for members of the British aristocracy while the

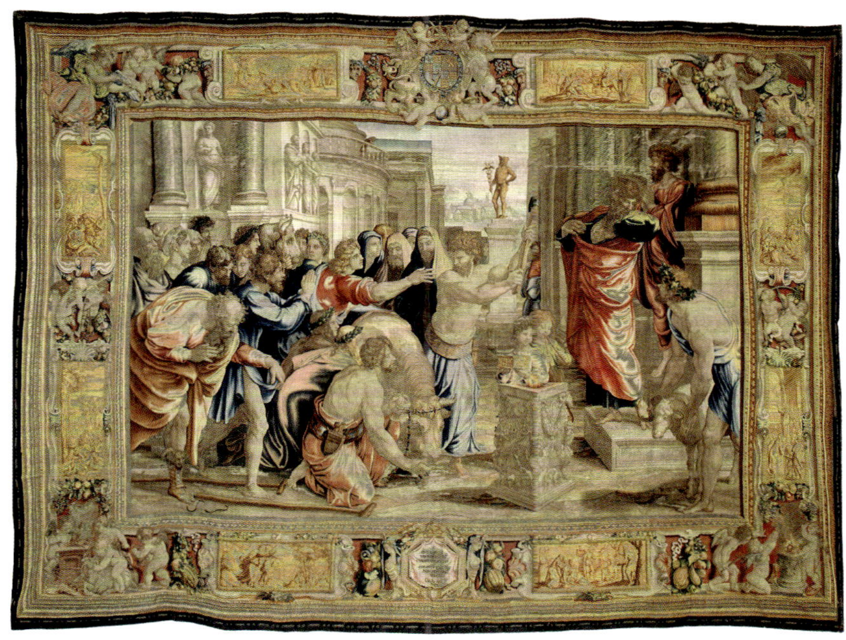

Cartoons themselves were put back into their crates and stored for another 80 years.[17] The first set woven for Charles I (*r.*1625–49) was not completed until 1640–1 and no record of the intended location for this series has survived.[18] It has been suggested that they were produced to furnish the newly rebuilt Banqueting House, begun by the British architect and designer Inigo Jones (1573–1652) in 1619. There, the tapestries would have complemented the ceiling painted by Rubens in about 1629–30.[19] Should this hypothesis be true, Raphael's designs would have been called upon for the exact same purpose a few decades apart.[20] The borders were not copied from the Renaissance set but specially designed by Cleyn. They

83

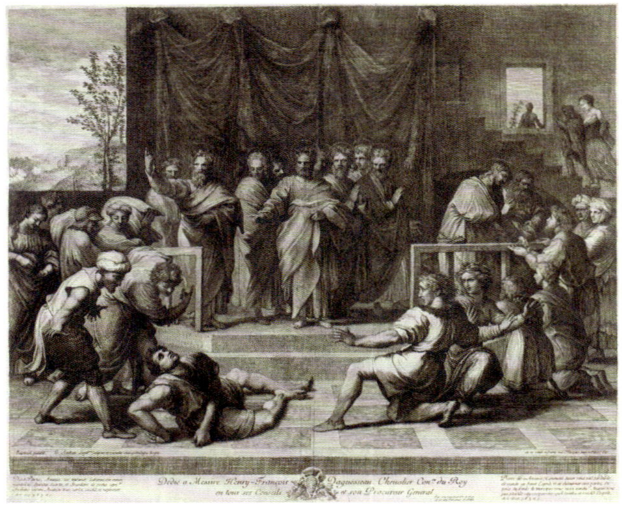

<< **53**
Gérard Audran (1640–1703),
after Raphael (1483–1520)
Death of Ananias, c.1700

Etching and engraving on paper,
58.5 x 69.6 cm (trimmed)
V&A: Dyce.2473

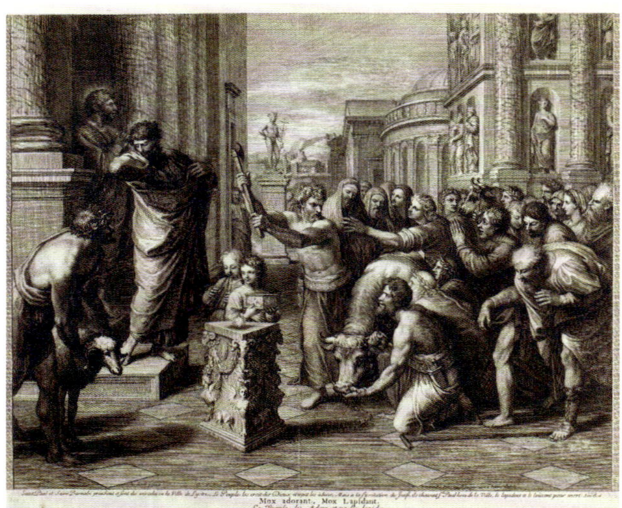

<< **54**
Gérard Audran (1640–1703),
after Raphael (1483–1520)
Sacrifice in Lystra, c.1700

Etching and engraving on paper,
56.8 x 67.5 cm (trimmed)
V&A: Dyce.2475

include putti with attributes of the theological virtues
and *trompe l'oeil* medallions surrounding Charles I's
coat of arms at the top centre (**52**).

Following the Civil War and and execution of
Charles I in 1649, the new republic led by Oliver Cromwell
(1599–1658) sold the late King's extraordinary collection
of works of arts to raise money for the new regime.
The Raphael Cartoons as well as Mantegna's painted
cycle of the *Triumphs of Caesar* (Hampton Court, Royal
Collection Trust), another Renaissance treasure, were kept

back, presumably on Cromwell's orders. The precious set of tapestries woven at Mortlake for Charles I, however, was sold and later acquired by Louis XIV of France. It is still in the collection of the Mobilier national in Paris. The Cartoons were returned to the Royal Household when the monarchy was restored in 1660, but it was only after the accession of William III in 1689 that they gradually regained their status as works of art in their own right.

As John Shearman pointed out in his seminal monograph on the Raphael Cartoons, 'it is always difficult to measure the penetration of a work of art into a national consciousness, and particularly difficult in the case of the English'.[21] The reception and appreciation of the Raphael Cartoons in England is indeed a very complicated story, which cannot be fully explored here. Nonetheless, one can note that this story broadly follows a three-stranded development: the display of the Cartoons themselves in various royal palaces where they were increasingly accessible to the public (to be seen within the wider demand for social and educational reforms),[22] their dissemination as engraved, painted or woven copies, and finally their place in artistic debate and related publications.

It was not until 1698 that William III entrusted Sir Christopher Wren (1632–1723) to design a specific gallery for the display of the Cartoons at Hampton Court.

Having been cut into strips for easier handling and storage, they were then reassembled, restored and made available for copying before the gallery was completed.[23] The Irish painter Charles Jervas was among the first to copy them. He later approached the 'peintre graveur' Gérard Audran (1640–1703), a member of the French Académie royale de peinture et de sculpture founded in 1648, to have his copies engraved for printing but death prevented Audran from engraving more than *The Death of Ananias* and *The Sacrifice at Lystra* (53, 54).[24] The

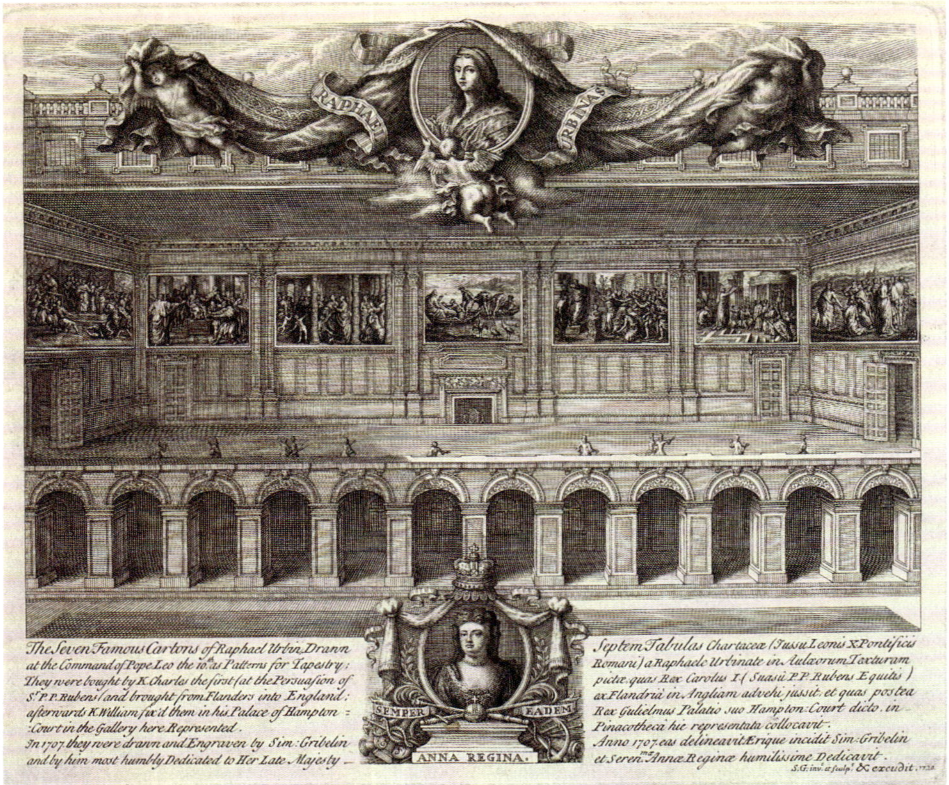

resulting prints are probably the first prints that can truly be said to be of the Cartoons. Jervas resorted to a French engraver because of the lack of expertise at the time in England. The British antiquarian and engraver George Vertue (1684–1756) noted that 'in London about 1700. the state of Print Engraveing on Copper was at a low ebb. [...] coud not be found any Master, as one may call so in London, because none of the others had any talent in drawing'.[25]

In 1707 another Frenchman, Simon Gribelin, who had moved to London in the early 1680s, produced the first full set of engravings after the Cartoons. His engravings show the compositions in reverse, therefore in the direction of the tapestries rather than the Cartoons. Engraving methods usually imply the reversal of the original design, like low-warp tapestry, but some engravers could anticipate this by cutting the image in reverse on the plate so that the printed copy appears in the same direction as the original. Only the frontispiece, which celebrates the Cartoons on display at Hampton Court, shows them in their original direction (55).[26] The reason for such a difference in treatment between the frontispiece and the plates is unknown, and there seems to have been no specific ruling as to how the Cartoons should be presented in print form, as earlier and later engravings attest. Furthermore, Gribelin altered the proportions of the Cartoons to produce a uniform set of prints. Nonetheless, according to Vertue, 'Mr. Griblins cartons in print from the pictures of Raphael were well receivd. & vast numbers of them (sold)'.[27]

Increased public access to the Cartoons from the last years of the seventeenth century prompted their recognition as 'national treasures' and the rise of an awareness of their art-historical significance in England while on the Continent, especially in Italy and France, Raphael had dominated much of the seventeenth century as a key figure and role model in artistic debate and practice alike.[28] The situation in England was rather different given the political upheavals and the civil war, which followed the deposition of Charles I. It was in this context that the English painter and collector Jonathan Richardson played an instrumental role in promoting Raphael's art in England, praising especially the Cartoons.[29] When the Vatican closed its doors in 1705 for a period of 20 years, Richardson could claim that:

'Hampton Court is the Great School of Rafaëlle!'[30]

The Cartoons had become the only monumental works by Raphael accessible (to a certain extent) in Europe.[31] Through their writings, the Richardsons, father and son, promoted Raphael's art as the apex of history painting,[32] going as far as ranking the Cartoons above the Vatican Stanze.[33]

While Richardson was embarking on his *Essay on the Theory of Painting* (1715), in which the Cartoons recur as outstanding examples of invention, expression, drawing, 'grace and greatness', the French engraver Nicolas Dorigny (1658–1746) was invited by a group of English patrons to produce another set of prints.[34] This new set was to be published in an elegant folio edition under the title *Pinacotheca Hamptoniana* and was presented to King George I (*r.*1714–27) in 1719 (**56**).[35] National pride in the Cartoons must have been by then at its climax since Dorigny was the first of only two men to be knighted for making specific prints. It is difficult to say at this stage whether the rise of art-theoretical discourse in England or the production of 'British' copies was the more influential, but they seem to have fuelled each other.

Copying famous works of art from the past has always played a key role in the formation of an artist.[36] The second step in the emulation of these models was to create compositions of one's own while drawing on

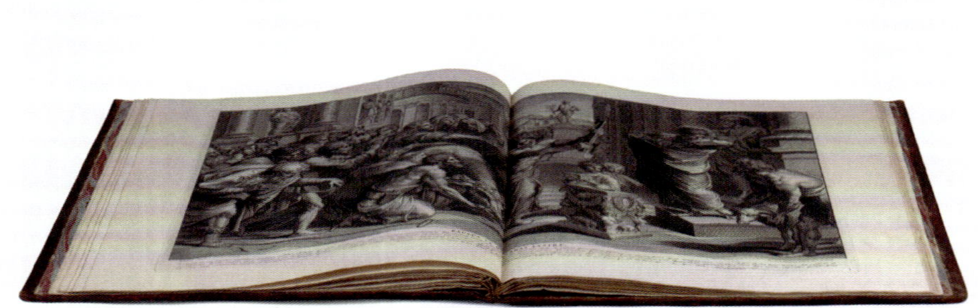

this visual repertory. It was therefore only a matter of time before the Cartoons fostered new inventions rather than fairly straightforward copies. This was masterfully exemplified by the painter James Thornhill, a life-long friend of Richardson, and one of the greatest exponents of the 'grand manner' in England. Echoes of the Raphael Cartoons can be seen in the eight scenes depicting the Acts of the Apostles, which Thornhill executed in the inner dome of St Paul's Cathedral between 1715 and 1717. These engaged with Raphael's models in a variety of ways from compositional formula to direct figural quotations.[37] William Hogarth (1697–1764), Thornhill's son-in-law, would make a similar attempt in his painting *Paul before Felix* (1748).[38]

A few years later, Thornhill copied the Cartoons on his own initiative. From 1729 to 1731, he produced at least three sets of copies and further detailed studies of heads, hands, limbs and architectural details (today gathered in two large albums, one of which is in the V&A) (57). These were most likely made with a view to developing a handbook for art students, following the same reasoning as Richardson in his *Essay on the whole art of criticism as it relates to painting and an argument in behalf of the science of the connoisseur* (1719), which promoted the use of copies for instruction.[39] Thornhill also had a philological approach, and tried to correct in his copies the many accidents and losses the Cartoons had endured over time.[40] His detailed studies were later engraved and

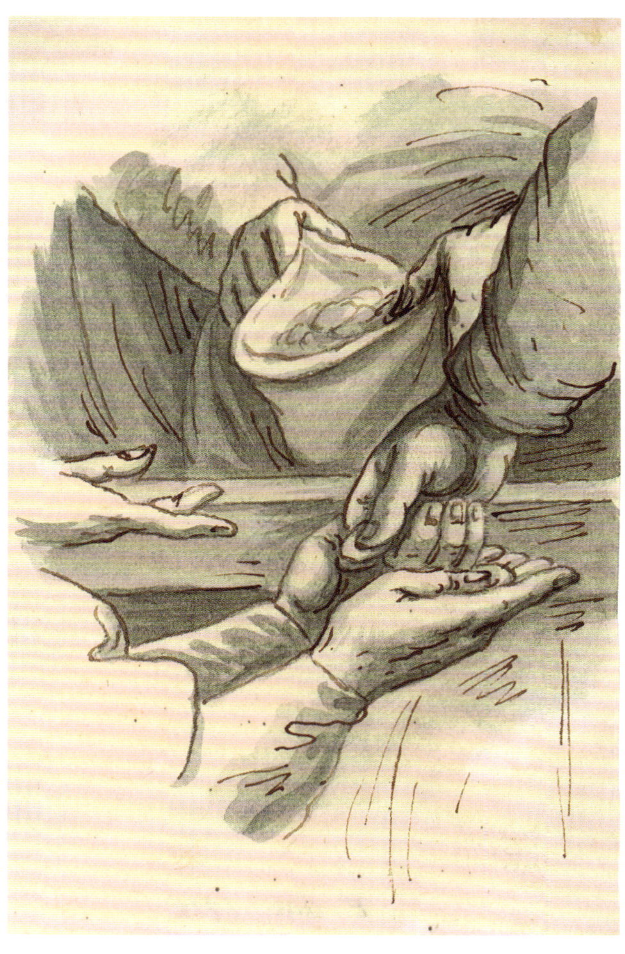

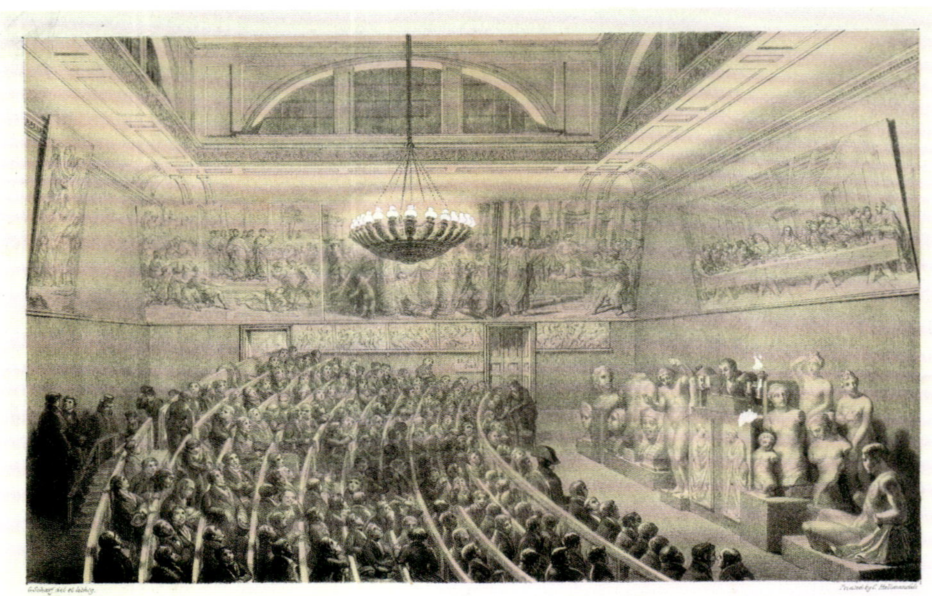

published in 1759 in a compilation titled *The School of Raphael* and described as follows:

> The student's guide to expression in historical painting illustrated by examples engraved by Duchange, and others, under the inspection of Sir Nicholas Dorigny, from his own drawings after the most celebrated heads in the Cartoons at the King's Palace; to which are now added the outlines of each head and also several plates of the most celebrated antique statues, skeletons, and anatomical figures engraved by an eminent artist; with instructions for young students in the art of designing and the passions as characterised by Raphael in the Cartoons described and explained by Benjamin Ralph.

This 1759 publication was in fact a revised and augmented edition of an album of prints made in 1722 after details from Dorigny's early copies.[41] Many editions of this book were published; the last as late as 1825.

Artistic teaching was an important subject from the early eighteenth century in England. It was a tradition

⌃ 58
George Johann Scharf
(1788–1860)
Lecture on Sculpture by Sir Richard Westmacott at the Royal Academy, Somerset House, 1830, 1850

Chalk-style lithotint, 20 x 31.6 cm
Royal Academy of Arts, London:
04/2743

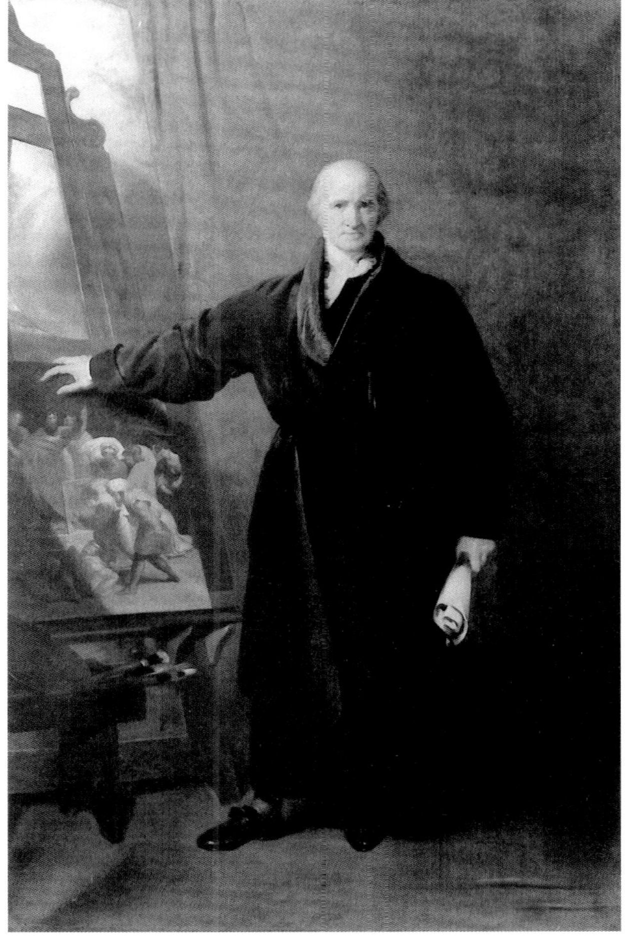

long established on the Continent, but Britain lacked a
proper institution until 1768, when the Royal Academy
was founded.[42] One of the later editions of *The School
of Raphael* had included Sir Joshua Reynolds' *Discourses
on Art*, a compilation of the lectures he delivered at
the Royal Academy between 1769 and 1790. In 1800
Thornhill's full-size copies were presented to the Royal
Academy for the use of students and for demonstration
in lectures (58).[43] The canonical example of the Raphael
Cartoons hardly ever wanes: in one of his last lectures,
on colour, given at the Royal Academy, its president
Benjamin West (1738–1820) still used a reduced copy
of *The Death of Ananias* (59) to illustrate his point.

His predecessor Sir Joshua Reynolds (1723–1792), the first president of the Royal Academy, similarly praised the power of invention demonstrated by Raphael in the Cartoons, despite his declared preference for Michelangelo.[44] Even painters who specialized in landscape, such as John Constable (1776–1837) and Joseph Mallord William Turner (1775–1851), copied the Cartoons: Constable made a copy in pen and ink of Dorigny's print after *Christ's Charge to Peter*,[45] while Turner made a diagram of the figure of St Paul in *Paul Preaching at Athens* for the purpose of his lectures as Professor of Perspective at the Royal Academy (**60**).[46]

Joseph Mallord William Turner (1775–1851)
Lecture Diagram: Geometry of the Figure of Raphael's 'Paul Preaching at Athens', c.1812–28

Watercolour on paper, 58.6 x 71 cm
Tate, London: Turner Bequest CXCV 168, D17139

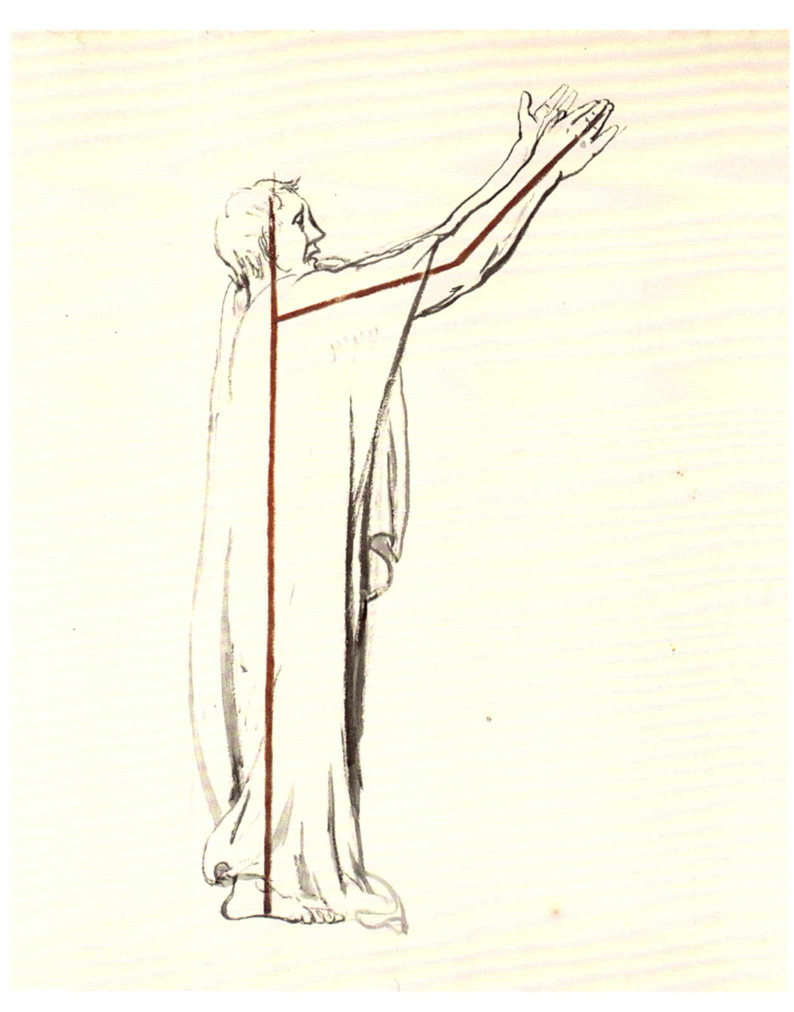

The art of Raphael continued to play a pivotal role in the formation of a British artistic identity and academic teaching until well into the nineteenth century. A short-lived disavowal, which goes hand in hand with the disapproval of the Academy's methods, was led by the Pre-Raphaelite Brotherhood, founded in 1848. The Pre-Raphaelites, whose principal members were William Holman Hunt (1827–1910), John Everett Millais (1829–1896) and Dante Gabriel Rossetti (1828–1882), declared their preference for a so-called 'primitive art' before Raphael went to Rome. In this, they were supported by the major art critic of the period, John Ruskin (1819–1900), who shared similar views.[47] Ruskin was also involved in the foundation of the Arundel Society (1848–97), whose purpose was to promote knowledge of the Old Masters through the dissemination, by subscription, of colour prints after their works. Mostly frescoes and fairly inaccessible works in Italy were prioritized, but copies after the Sistine Chapel's tapestries, corresponding to the missing designs from the Raphael Cartoons, are also to be found.[48] The Arundel Society especially favoured the making of hand-drawn copies, later reproduced as chromolithographs and engravings, because they were felt to be more genuine and closer to the original media. However, the invention of photography in the 1830s would eventually supplant these earlier preferred methods of reproducing the Cartoons.[49]

In the year 2020 when we commemorate the 500th anniversary of the death of Raphael, the V&A, home to the Cartoons for the past 155 years, embarked on a new reproduction project with the pioneering technique of three-dimensional scanning. Combined with other types of imagery, such as infra-red reflectography, these new techniques offer non-invasive methods of studying these canonical works of art by allowing us to look beneath the visible layers of paint and discover Raphael's creative processes. Thus coloured images in high resolution reveal the extraordinarily fresh palette used by Raphael to harmonize his designs with the existing decoration of the Sistine Chapel. This cutting-edge technology allows us to enjoy the extraordinary achievements of an artist of genius while enabling the V&A to record and preserve these outstanding national treasures for future generations.

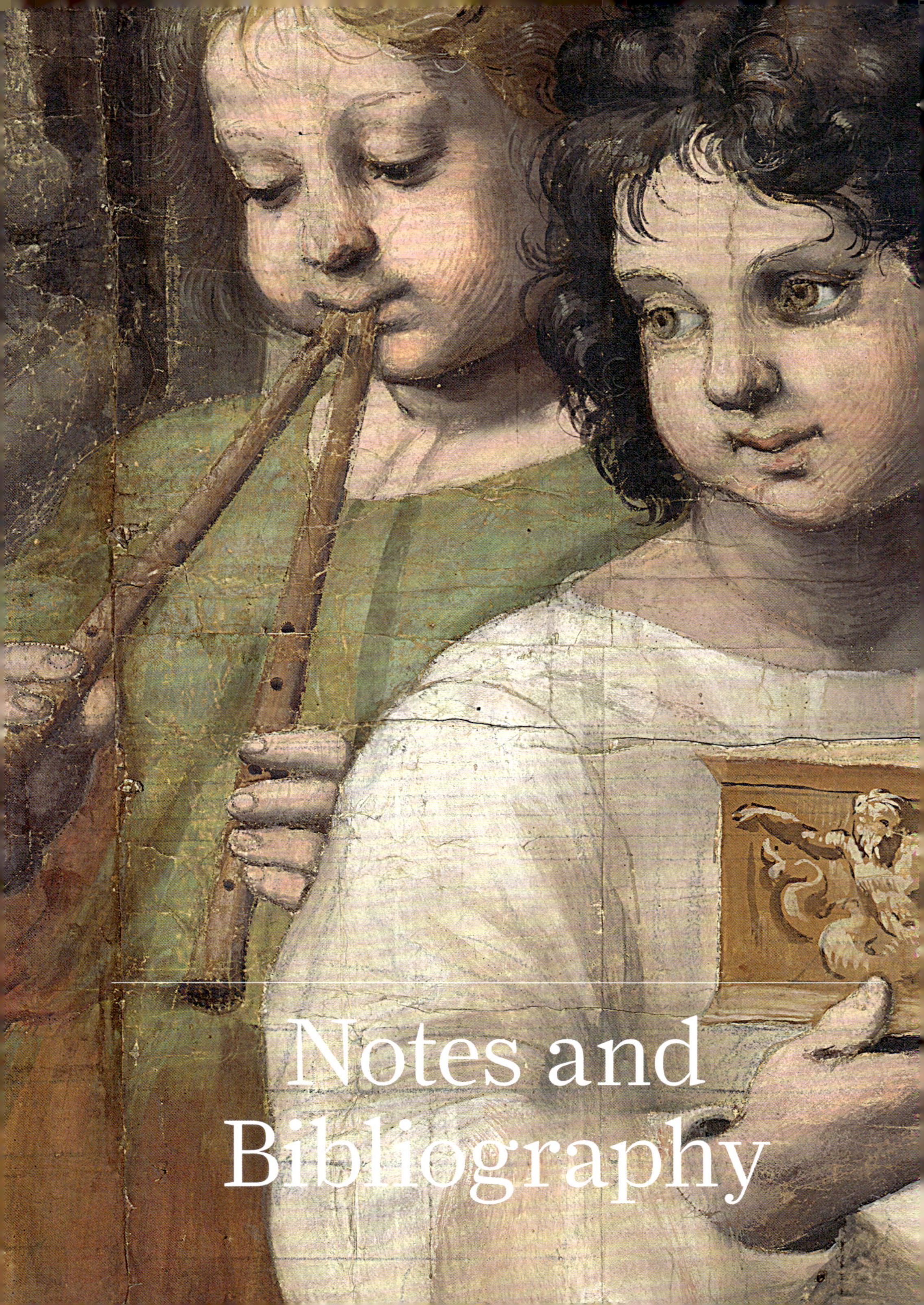
Notes and
Bibliography

Notes

The Museum Story

1 Ruland 1876, p. XII.

2 Becker and Ruland 1863, pp. 27–39, esp. p. 28.

3 Cole 1853, p. 30.

4 Montagu 1986, pp. 167–83. DOI: 10.1080/01973762.1986.9659086, repr. in Roberts 1995, pp. 37–57.

5 Bryant 2019, p. 50. These are now in the Photographic Collection, accessible to the public in the Prints and Drawings Study Room and via the online catalogue.

6 Physick 1975, pp. 6–7.

7 *Report from the Select Committee on the South Kensington Museum: Together with the Proceedings of the Committee, Minutes of Evidence, and Appendix* (London 1860): 'Henry Cole, Minutes of the Committee's report on 5 July 1860', p. 18.

8 The cabinet was supplied by J.C. Grace before the Prince's death. See Clayton 2010, pp. 176–7.

9 Shearman 1972, pp. 157–8.

10 Ruland 1876, p. 8.

11 Ibid.

12 Windsor, Royal Archives, RA/PPTO/PP/QV/MAIN/1875/18811: Letter, 8 April 1875, from Henry Cole to Sir Thomas Biddulph.

13 Ibid.

14 Ruland 1866, p. 11.

15 Ibid., p. 12.

16 Shearman 1972, p. 159.

17 Physick 1982, p. 270.

18 See Plesters 1990.

19 See Fermor and Derbyshire 1998, pp. 236–50. See also Browne and Evans 2010.

The Making of the Cartoons

1 For an image of the Sistine Chapel with the tapestries hanging, see p. 51.

2 Vasari 1963, vol. 2, p. 242; Vasari 1966–87, vol. IV, pp. 201–2: 'venne volontà al Papa di far panni d'arazzi ricchissimi d'oro e di seta in filatici'.

3 The most famous composition of the series, *The School of Athens*, was copied numerous times and became a great source of inspiration for the generations of artists to follow. A full-size copy by the German painter Anton Raphael Mengs (1728–1779), originally commissioned by the Duke of Northumberland, hangs in the Cast Court (Gallery 46B) at the V&A (P.36–1926).

4 Vasari 1963, vol. 2, p. 242; Vasari 1966–87, vol. IV, p. 201.

5 Golzio 1936, pp. 38 and 51; Shearman 2003, vol. 1, 1515/6, p. 205 and 1516/31, p. 271.

6 Vasari 1963, vol. 2, p. 242. Vasari 1966–87, vol. IV, p. 202 'Raffae lo fece in propria forma e grandezza di tutti, di sua mano, i cartoni coloriti, i quai furono mandati in Fiandra a tessersi, e finiti i panni, vennero a Roma'.

7 Vasari 1981, vol. I, pp. 174–5.

8 Bambach 1999, p. 294.

9 See Clayton 1999, cats 25–7, pp. 99–112.

10 Raphael, Modello for *The Conversion of the Proconsu.*, c.1515, metalpoint, brown wash, white heightening and later pen and ink, over stylus and black chalk on pale buff prepared paper, 26.9 x 35.4 cm, Royal Collection, Windsor: RCIN 912750, RL12750; see Joannides 1983, cats 355–66, for the preparatory drawings for the Sistine Chapel Cartoons.

11 Raphael, Study for *The Miraculous Draught of Fishes*, c.1515, pen, brush and brown ink, brown wash with white heightening over black chalk on paper, 22.9 x 32.7 cm, Albertina, Vienna: 192r. This sheet was alternatively attributed to Raphael and to his close collaborators Giulio Romano and Giovan Francesco Penni. It was recently published as fully autograph by Ben Thomas in *Raphael: The Drawings*, exh. cat., Ashmolean Museum, Oxford (Oxford 2017), cat. 103.

12 Raphael, *Figure of a Woman Looking to the Right with her Left Arm Stretched Out*, c.1515, pen and brown ink over black chalk on paper, 10 x 13.8 cm, Staatlische Graphische Sammlung München: 6235 Z; see Joannides 1983, cat. 355, p. 222.

13 Vasari 1981, vol. 1, p. 170.

14 Martin Clayton believes it is by Raphael and not Penni – or Giovanni da Udine as otherwise suggested by Nesselrath 2019, pp. 314–16. See Clayton 1999, cat. 25, pp. 99–103. Furthermore, the technique employed on the recto of this drawing is similar to that of the drawing in Vienna: the two sheets are of approximately the same size and share the same painterly employment of pen and brown ink over traces of black and red chalks, highlighted with white on a washed paper. They provide us with two alternative solutions firmly developed for the same Cartoon, attesting to Raphael's power of invention in his search for perfection.

15 Raphael, Fragment of a study for *Christ's Charge to Peter*, c.1515, stylus and red chalk on paper, 25.3 x 13.4 cm, Musée du Louvre, Paris: Inv. 3854; Raphael, *Eight Apostles*, c.1515, stylus and red chalk on paper, cut in two pieces and rejoined, 8.1 x 23.2 cm, Woodner Collections, National Gallery of Art, Washington: 1993.51.2; Raphael, Study of figures for *The Sacrifice at Lystra*, c.1515, leadpoint highlighted with white on a prepared blue paper, 24.8 x 39.2 cm, Musée du Louvre, Paris: RF 38813 recto.

16 Raphael, Counterproof of *Christ's Charge to Peter*, c.1515, red chalk on paper, 25.8 x 37.5 cm, Royal Collection, Windsor: RL 12751.

17 Attr. to Giovan Francesco Penni, Study for *Paul Preaching at Athens*, 1515–16, pen and brown ink, brown wash, black chalk, heightened with white, squared for transfer, 27 x 40 cm, Musée du Louvre, Paris: Inv. 3884 recto; Cordellier and Py 1992, pp. 263–84.

18 Vasari 1981, vol. I, p. 122. Giovanni da Udine, *Studies of Birds*, pen and brown ink, brown wash highlighted with white on paper (whereabouts unknown), reproduced in Shearman 1972, fig. 40.

19 Vasari 1981, vol. I, p. 301. These unfortunately do not survive.

20 Vasari 1963, vol. 2, p. 242; Vasari 1966–87, vol. IV, p. 202. Fermor 1996.

21 Campbell 2002, pp. 45–6 and 133.

22 See for instance the St Cecilia altarpiece (oil on wood transferred to canvas, 236 x 149 cm, Pinacoteca Nazionale, Bologna, Inv. 577) and *Christ Falls on the Way to Calvary* (*Lo Spasimo di Sicilia*), a large altarpiece for the Church of Santa Maria dello Spasimo in Palermo (oil on wood transferred to canvas, 318 x 229 cm, today in Prado Museum, Madrid: P000298), both executed in about 1515–16, as well as the *Transfiguration* altarpiece (tempera grassa on wood, 410 x 279 cm, Musei Vaticani, Rome, Cat. 40333), made 1516–20.

23 See for instance a 3D model of the vaulted hall in the V&A collection 334:1 to 6–1889.

24 Vasari 1963, vol. 3, pp. 240–1; Vasari 1966–87, vol. IV, pp. 197–8.

25 Vasari 1963, vol. 3, p. 104; Vasari 1966–87, vol. V, p. 68.

26 On Raphael and antique Rome see Faietti and Lafranconi 2020, pp. 192–4 and cat. V.22–9.

27 Dacos 1980, pp. 61–99, esp. pp. 79–88; Nello Forti Grazzini, 'Arazzi di Bruxelles in Italia, 1440–1535' in Castelnuovo 1990, pp. 35–73, esp. pp. 56–7.

28 Parma 2001; Campbell 2002, pp. 341–63.

29 See Alessandra Rodolfo's chapter in this volume.

30 Frimmel 1888, p. 104. On the influence of Raphael's design on Venetian painters see Ballarin 1967, pp. 96 ff.

31 Armenini 1587, vol. II, pp. 101–4.

32 Vasari 1981, vol. VII, p. 161.

33 Another piece of evidence is the inscription on the base of the Proconsul's pedestal in *The Conversion of the Proconsul*, which normally reads from left to right (and not backwards as it would in a template), indicating that the Cartoon was not used on the loom but probably intended to be displayed in due course.

34 Two further copies survive however, much damaged, in the National Gallery of Ireland (NGI 171 and 172). Shearman believed them to be of Flemish origin (Shearman 1972, p. 145); but with no information on their provenance they may also be much later copies. Further investigation is needed to ascertain their origins. See McParland 2019, pp. 325–32.

35 Perronet 1995–8, cats 15–17, pp. 76–80.

36 On this method of transfer see Bambach-Cappel 1988, vol. I, part I, pp. 1–176. Sometimes

a few sheets of paper could be pricked together, so as to produce several sets in one go. See Saint-Aubin 1770, p. 5.

37   Cicogna 1860 (IX), p. 405: 'Adi 27 dicembre 1519, Roma. Queste feste di Natale il Papa messe fuori in Capella 7 pezzi di razzo perché l'ottavo non era fornito fatti in ponente, che furono giudicati la piu bella cosa, che sia stata fatta in eo genere a nostri giorni [...]'; Smith 1993, pp. 48–60.

38   Shearman 1972, p. 13, no. 77; Campbell 2002, p. 187.

39   Vasari 1963, vol. 2, p. 242; Vasari 1966–87, vol. IV, p. 202.

Raphael's Tapestries Past and Present

1   Pastor 1905, p. 117.

2   Archives in the possession of the Bini Smaghi Bellarmini family, who sponsored their cataloguing by Alessio Caporali in October 2012. Unfortunately, it has not been possible to access the archives to verify the information given in Caporali 2014 and Caporali 2017.

3   Already in Caporali 2014 and with further details in Caporali 2017; http://hdl.handle.net/2158/1075933 (accessed 20 May 2020).

4   Caporali (Caporali 2017, p. 326) relates a *motu proprio* from Leo X (dating from the first semester of 1519) with the Busini Strozzi institutions, Bini and the *dilecto filio* Petro Va[n] Aelst that mentions the delivery of gold threads (*consegna di filato d'oro*) to Pieter van Aelst and its payment to the merchant-weaver; De Strobel 2020 – Regesto documentario, p. 297, reports a similar *motu proprio* (from the Vatican Secret Archives) with the date 23 June 1520 and hypothesizes that the payment relates to the *Grottesche* set as per the dimensions of the tapestries, see De Strobel 2020, p. 23. According to Caporali (Caporali 2017, p. 327) the examination of the payments made between 1518 and 1521 suggests that Bernardo Bini, in those years, made an advanced payment of 36,430 gold ducats of Camera for the making of non-specified Flemish tapestries which probably include the Acts of the Apostles set. Caporali remarks that the documentation is lacunary and difficult to interpret (oral communication to the author).

5   Gaye 1839–40, II, p. 222 quotes a similar payment, '1518, 18 Giugno. Ducati 1000 pagati a Pietro Loroi fiammingo a buon conto d'arazerie; sono ducati di Camera', from a volume of Conti, bilanci ed altre partite atterenti a Leone X' of which no trace remairs. Shearman 2003, p. 335, interprets the document as a possible partial payment for the Acts of the Apostles set.

6   This odd spelling is interpreted by Caporali as Van Aelst bearing in mind that the Flemish artist is cited as 'Pietro tappezziere' or 'Pietro Vanagher', recipient of further payments for Flemish tapestries. This might result from the incorrect transcription of the name Van Edigen or d'Enghien.

7   BAV, Vat. Lat. 12416. Paris de Grassis, *Diario di Leone X*, f. 366r.

8   Ibid.

9   As Pietro Aretino described it in his letter addressed to Marcantonio Michiel, see Aretino 1999.

10   Venice, BCorr, MS Cicogna 2848. Marcantonio Michiel, *Diario*, ff. 314v–315r; Shearman 2003, 1519/66, p. 491 with previous bibliography.

11   ASMn, Archivio Gonzaga, 864, f. 561r. *Lettera di Francesco Chiericati da Roma a Isabella d'Este a Mantova*, Shearman 2003, 1520/68, p. 631.

12   All ten tapestries feature in the inventory of 7 September 1518, with a note on 17 December 1521 (ASR, Camerale I, Inventari, 1557, reg. 1). Shearman, who notes different handwritings in the document and attributes the registration of the tapestries to the third and last, hypothesizes the arrival of the tapestries in 1520 at the earliest and 1521 at the latest: see Shearman 2003, 1519/55, pp. 479–81.

13   White and Shearman 1958; Shearman 1972, pp. 21–44; Mancinelli 1982, p. 53; Gilbert 1987; Campbell 2002, pp. 200–1; Shearman 2003, p. 293; De Strobel and Nesselrath 2010, pp. 26–9; De Strobel and Nesselrath 2020, pp. 68–9.

14   Shearman 1972, pp. 21–44 followed by Weddigen 1993/1999, pp. 268–73; Rohlmann 2003, pp. 95–108; Weddingen 2006, 32 Ritual, Messliturgie/Maiestas.

15   Such installation implied the story of St Paul on the south wall and the story of St Peter on the north wall while *The Stoning of Stephen* and *The Miraculous Draught of Fishes*, according to Shearman, to be set on the altar wall, could not be installed because of *The Last Judgement* painted on that wall. The only tapestry outside the screen, according to Shearman, moved after the creation of the tapestries (Shearman 1972, pp. 21–44), was *Paul Preaching at Athens*, displayed in the part of the chapel reserved for the lay people.

16   The one-evening display of the Pauline cycle on the north wall and another two (*Christ's Charge to Peter* and *The Healing of the Lame Man*) on the south wall was made on the occasion of the press conference for the exhibition *Raphael, Cartoons and Tapestries for the Sistine Chapel* (Victoria and Albert Museum, London, 8 September–18 October 2010), which presented side by side the Cartoons and four tapestries for the Sistine Chapel set (*The Miraculous Draught of Fishes, Christ's Charge to Peter, The Healing of the Lame Man* and *The Sacrifice at Lystra*).

17   On the moving of the screen see Steinmann 1897; Shearman 1972; Nesselrath 2003, pp. 36–7; Nesselrath 2010, pp. 23–4, De Strobel and Nesselrath 2020, pp. 70–6.

18   De Strobel and Nesselrath 2020, pp. 76–7.

19   Ibid., p. 78.

20   Tav. III proposed reconstruction of the Sistine Chapel for the mass of St Stephen, graphic design by Paola Brunori and Chiara Cortesi in De Strobel 2020, vol. II.

21   Tav. V proposed reconstruction of the original installation including all tapestries. South wall proposed reconstruction by Paola Brunori and Chiara Cortesi in De Strobel 2020, vol. II.

22   Caporali 2017, p. 324.

23   Shearman (Shearman 2003, 1521/39, pp. 708–9) identified Belzer as 'Giovanni de Belza fiamingho et preposito cameracense, scriptor apostolico'; he is, according to De Strobel and Nesselrath, the German banker Johann Welser, from a family of bankers from Augsburg. See De Strobel 2020, pp. 65, 299–300, 307, 309.

24   ASV, Camera Apostolica, Diversa Cameralia 70, f. 119v in De Strobel and Nesselrath 2010, p. 31; De Strobel 2020 – Regesto documentario D16, 17 December 1521.

25   BAV, Arch. Chigi, 11458, f. 59r. De Strobel 2020 – Regesto documentario D17, 26 December 1521, pp. 309–10.

26   Shearman 2003, 1521/38, with previous bibliography.

27   ABSB, Bini, Attività Finanziarie, sez. I, IV cc. 6r–8r, cc. 18r–19r. 'Nota delle gioie e argienti [...] appartenenti alla Sede Apostolica' in Caporali 2017, p. 58, note 71.

28   ASMo, Archivio Estense, Ambasciatori, Roma, b. 28, 187.IV.23. Report by Ludovico Cati, ambassador for the Este family in Rome. Pastor 1956, IV, 2, p. 50, note 3; De Strobel 2020 – Regesto documentario D20, 2 September 1523, p. 310.

29   Sanudo, *Diarii*, XLV, 418; see Shearman 2003, 1527/6, p. 825.

30   Shearman 2003, p. 825; D26. 18 June 1527 (with reference to 12 May 1527).

31   Acquired by Marco Antonio Contarini, called Captain Cacciadiavolo by the King of Tunis, who had obtained them from the Turkish pirates who had attacked the ship that was supposed to deliver them to Isabella d'Este in Mantua. Shearman 2003, nn. 1527/7, 1528/4, 1528/6, 1528/7, 1528/10; De Strobel 2020 – Regesto documentario, cat. 7, *The Conversion of Saul*, p. 18.

32   Inventario 23–8 April 1555, ASR, Camerale I, 1557, reg. 3, ff. 105, De Strobel 2020 – Regesto documentario D56, 23–8 April 1555, pp. 325–6.

33   Camillo Tutini, *Discorsi dei sette officii del Regno*, Roma, 1666, pp. 176–7, last work of the Neapolitan. Exemplar in BAV, Ottoboniani Latini, ms. 2700, c. 17r. See Giuliano 2017, p. 44.

34   Bazzano 2011, s. v.

35   Except for *The Conversion of Saul, Paul Preaching at Athens* and *The Conversion of the Proconsul*. There are no records of the other seven tapestries after the Sack of Rome until 1536, when they appeared again in the first known inventory of the Floreria.

36 ASF, Carteggio Mediceo, filza 5089, doc. 268, Heikamp 1969, p. 74, note 35; De Strobel – Regesto documentario D58, 27 December 1577, p. 327.

37 See Fagiolo 1997a.

38 *Relatione Delle Cerimonie, e apparato della Basilica di San Pietro nella canonizatione de' gloriosi santi Pietro D'Alcantara e Maria Maddalena de' Pazzi fatte dalla Santità di N. Sig. Clemente Nono il di XXVIII. Aprile M.D.C.LXIX*, in Fagiolo 1997a, vol. 1, p. 472.

39 Fototeca Zeri, scheda 62823; Arisi 1986, p. 433, no. 406; Fagiolo 1997b, p. 143.

40 This rare image is known from an early photograph preserved in the Zeri Foundation Photo Archive.

41 *Distinta relazione* … in Fagiolo 1997b, pp. 143–4. See also *Diario ordinario* 5061, Rome, 27 December 1749, pp. 10–12.

42 Moroni 1841a, IX, p. 49.

43 Moroni 1841b, IX, pp. 284–6.

44 Turriziani 2020, no. 5, p. 3.

45 Goethe 1983, p. 389. Goethe was in Italy from 1786 to 1788.

46 Pietrangeli 1985, p. 124, note 61. For the Paris exhibition see Gastinel-Coural 1996, p. 1998. I should like to thank Morgane Lucquet-Laforgue for drawing this information to my attention.

47 ASMV, b. 4, fasc. 6, n. 33, minutes of a letter from Monsignor Mazzone. De Strobel 2020 – Regesto documentario D103, 12 May 1815, p. 354.

48 24 December 1824, Apertura della Roma, Basilica di S. Pietro. 'Il portico della Basilica era abbellito da preziosi tessuti e dai pregevoli arazzi di Raffaello'; see Fagiolo 1997b, p. 306.

49 *Diario di Roma* 102, Rome, Wednesday 21 December 1836, p. 4.

The Cartoons at Hampton Court Palace

Some of the research presented in this chapter was originally published in two articles for the *Journal of the History of Collections*: see Dolman 2017 and Dolman 2018.

1 An order to deliver the 'large case' of the Cartoons to Kinnersley was sent on 11 March 1689: The National Archives (NA) LC 5/149, p. 17. Lord Chamberlain's Warrant Book, 1689. Excerpt from the diary of Huygens for 7 May 1689 translated and quoted in Dekker 2013, pp. 77–8. Huygens also recorded another display of the Cartoons 'for some admirers' at the Banqueting House on 16 December 1690.

2 According to Huygens' diary, Norris saw the Cartoons at the Banqueting House on 26 May 1689. Walton received payments for repairing the Cartoons: NA T 38/735, 7 September 1691 & 10 July 1693; Treasury cashbooks of payments by Henry Guy. George Vertue suggested Cooke had also been involved in the process: Vertue 1929–30, vol. 1, p. 94. Cooke certainly copied the Cartoons: NA LC 5/152, p.25, 27 July 1697; Lord Chamberlain's Warrant Book, 1697–1700. Jervas was likewise employed: NA LC 5/151, f.375, 24 July 1694; Lord Chamberlain's Warrant Book, 1691–6.

3 The workmen's accounts for 1697: NA WORK 5/49, f.300–22, June-November 1697; Office of Works Accounts 1697–8. Charles Hatton's letter published in Thompson 1878 vol. 2, p. 229.

4 Simon Thurley provides a comprehensive account of the rebuilding of Hampton Court under William III and Mary II, see Thurley 2003. Huygens records Queen Mary's interest in the Cartoons moving to Hampton Court in his diary entry for 7 May 1691. Talman's letter: British Library, Additional MS 20101, f.69.

5 For a discussion of William III's involvement in the selection of art for Hampton Court, see Jenkins 1994, pp. 4–9. Also *Paintings from England: William III and the Royal Collections*, exh. cat., Mauritshuis (The Hague 1988).

6 Blackmore 1703.

7 Steele 1711.

8 See the last chapter in this volume.

9 Early guidebooks to eulogize

the Cartoons include Defoe 1724 and Bickham 1742. *The Idler*, 29 September 1759 (London 1761), vol. 2, no. 76, pp. 130–5.

10 Slaughter's instructions: NA AO 1/420/200; Account Roll of the Treasury of the Chamber, 1762–3. The Surveyor's payments for removing the Cartoons in December 1763: NA LC 5/168; Fees Book, 1761–5. Walpole's letter to George Montagu commenting on the stripping of the older palaces is dated 25 May 1762: Lewis 1937–83, vol. 10, p. 33. The surviving plans showing the arrangement of pictures at Buckingham House are published and discussed in Russell 1987, pp. 524–31.

11 Boydell 1764. Richard Dalton's account of the Cartoons in *The Gentleman's Magazine and Historical Chronicle* (October 1787), vol. 57, pt 2, p. 853. Wilkes' rant is published in Cobbett 1806–20, vol. 19 (1814), cols 190ff.

12 Volkmann's account appeared in *Neueste Reisen durch England* (Leipzig 1782), vol. 2, p. 361, and is translated and quoted by Shearman 1972. Walpole's unsuccessful visit is dated 25 June 1783[?]: Walpole 1928, p. 78.

13 Farington 1978–84, vol. 6, p. 2399; 30 August 1804.

14 Ibid., vol. 14, p. 4943; 13 December 1816.

15 Ibid., vol. 14, pp. 4575–6; 28 August 1814.

16 Pope 1960–3, vol. 4, p. 146. *Report from the Select Committee on Arts and their Connexion with Manufactures* (16 August 1836), p. x.

17 For a wider discussion about the events leading to the free public opening of Hampton Court in 1838, and the history of the public picture galleries at the palace, see Dolman 2018, pp. 217–33, and Dolman 2017, pp. 271–90.

18 Uwins' unsuccessful attempts to secure funding for the Cartoons' conservation: NA WORK 19/71; collected papers relating to pictures at royal palaces, 1849–55.

19 The painted copies are on loan from the Ashmolean Museum, Oxford. They are attributed either to William III's artist, Henry Cooke, *c.*1697, or to the Dutch artist Isaac Vogelsang, working for James-Christopher LeBlon in the late 1720s.

The Afterlife of the Cartoons

1 Oberhuber 1984, p. 337.

2 Vasari 1966–87, V, p. 10; Oberhuber 1984, pp. 333–42. See also *The Healing of the Lame Man* etched by Parmigianino, *c.*1527–30, which may record, in reverse, a lost drawing by the master (an example is in the Royal Collection: RCIN 853106). In this way, some of these prints inform us of the creative process at work during the making of the Cartoons, as they register intermediary phases; see for instance *Raffaello in Vaticano* (Rome 1984), p. 365 (137), p. 366 (138), p. 367 (139a and b).

3 Vasari 1963, vol. 3, pp. 74–5 (modified by the author); Vasari 1966–87, vol. V, pp. 10–11: 'avendo Raffaello fatto per la capella del Papa tutti i cartoni dei panni d'arazzo, che furono poi tessuti di seta e d'oro, con istorie di San Piero, S. Paulo e S. Stefano, Marcantonio intagliò la predicazzione di San Paulo, la Lapidazione di Santo Stefano, et il rendere il lume al cieco: le quali stampe furono tanto belle per l'invenzione di Raffaello, per la grazia del disegno, per la diligenza et intaglio di Marcantonio, che non era possibile veder meglio'.

4 Vasari 1966–87, vol. IV, p. 190. Vasari 1963, vol. 2, p. 237. See also Raphael, *La fornarina, c.*1520, oil on wood, 87 x 63 cm, Palazzo Barberini, Rome: 2333.

5 See Brooks 2015, p. 88.

6 See for instance Nicolas Poussin's three large scenes from the New Testament of the mid-1650s. *Christ and the Woman Taken in Adultery* (1653) and *The Death of Sapphira* (1654) are in the Musée du Louvre, Paris (Inv. 7282 and Inv. 7286). The third painting, *Saints Peter and John Healing the Lame Man* (1655), is in the Metropolitan Museum of Art, New York (24.45.2). See also in 1649, Eustache Le Sueur (1616–1655), *The Preaching of Saint Paul at Ephesus* (Musée du Louvre, Paris: Inv. 8020), which combines elements from *The Sacrifice at Lystra* and *The Healing of the Lame Man*; a preparatory sketch is in the National Gallery, London (NG6299). His second series of the Seven Sacraments remains the most profound testimony to the power of Raphael's Cartoons.

7 Nicola Pellipario, Polychrome maiolica plate depicting *The Conversion of the Proconsul*, Urbino, *c.*1530, Civici Musei del castello Sforzesco, Milan;

Polychrome maiolica plate depicting *The Healing of the Lame Man*, Pesaro, *c*.1540–50, V&A: C.2251–1910; Patanazzi workshop, polychrome maiolica plate depicting *Paul Preaching at Athens*, late 16th century, Pinacoteca e Musei Civici, Pesaro; Enamel platter depicting *The Death of Ananias*, Limoges, *c*.1580, Los Angeles County Museum; Plaquette by unknown artist depicting *The Miraculous Draught of Fishes*, *c*.1887, Vatican Museums, Rome (MV_70530_2_1).

8   Campbell 2007, p. 267.

9   Supposedly destroyed in Berlin during the Second World War (1945), a set of photographs survived in the Hunter Archives in the Getty Resource Collection.

10   Campbell 2007, pp. 274–5.

11   During the seventeenth century, we find hardly any new prints after the Cartoons, and the tendency seems to have been to reprint the 16th-century blocks and plates, such as Ugo da Carpi's woodcut of *The Miraculous Draught of Fishes*, reissued by Andrea Andreani in 1609 (see V&A: E.493–1925).

12   Charles, Prince of Wales, 28 March 1623, Letter in *Affairs of Charles*, p. 4; see Shearman 1972, p. 146, note 70.

13   See Rubens, *The Discovery of Calipso*, *c*.1600, pen and ink on paper, Kupertischkabinett, Berlin (3239), which includes a study after the figure of the Proconsul; and also Rubens, *The Miraculous Draught of Fishes*, 1618–19, oil sketch, National Gallery, London (NG680), which shows direct inspiration from the Cartoon. A full copy after Raphael's *Paul Preaching at Athens*, was attributed to Rubens (*c*.1600, pen and ink on paper, Uppsala Universitetsbibliothek: 9345), see Jaffé 1967, p. 102; Shearman 1972, p. 147 – but this attribution has since been debated by scholars: see Jeremy Wood, 'Rubens and Raphael: The Designs for the Tapestries in the Sistine Chapel' in *Munuscula amicorum. Contributions on Rubens and his Colleagues in honour of Hans Vlieghe*, ed. Katlijne Van der Stighelen (Turnhout 2006), vol. I, pp. 259–82.

14   Piero Boccardo identified the seller in Genoa as one Andrea Imperiale in Boccardo 2006, p. 182.

15   *Paul in Prison*, which is the smallest of the series and narrow (479 x 128 cm), seems to have been woven only once for the original set, no doubt because it is site specific to the Sistine Chapel. See Alessandra Rodolfo's chapter in this volume.

16   Thomson 1914, pp. 72–3.

17   For instance, a set for the Earl of Pembroke (examples are in the collection of the Duke of Buccleuch, Boughton House, Northamptonshire) was woven in the same period as well as another for the Duke of Devonshire (three of which are on public display at Chatsworth); another set was woven in the 1660s for the Earl of Holland (now Mobilier national, Paris). The manufactory's activity subsequently decreased leading to its definitive closure in 1704.

18   Wyld 2018, p 190.

19   Palme 1957, pp. 27–8, 273–82.

20   Their significance for a Protestant monarch follows the same reasoning as that behind the commission of the set by King Henry VIII. The cycle was re-purposed to support the King of England as Head of the English Church, who had a special devotion for the Apostles Peter and Paul.

21   Shearman 1972, p. 152.

22   See Brett Dolman's chapter in this volume.

23   George Vertue's Note Book A. F. [British Museum, Add. MS. 23,076], *The Volume of the Walpole Society* 22 (1933), pp. 15, 42; www.jstor.org/stable/41830356 (accessed 3 March 2020).

24   Jervas copied them for the print collector Dr George Clarke, of All Souls, Oxford: Vertue's Note Book 1933, p. 42. Clarke was an important figure in the introduction of Renaissance architectural forms to Oxford. See H. Colvin, *A Biographical Dictionary of British Architects* (New Haven and London 2008), pp. 253–5.

25   Vertue's Note Book 1933, p. 7.

26   Gribelin's preparatory drawings for the engravings are in the Royal Collection (RCINs 917313–21).

27   Vertue's Note Book 1933, p. 7. The set was republished by John Bowles in 1720.

28   *See Raphael et l'art français* (Paris 1983); Fagiolo and Madonna 1990; Rosenberg 1995.

29   Shearman 1972, p. 151; Gibson-Wood 2000,

pp. 138–221. He probably copied them as soon as they became available in Hampton Court, making negative comments on Dorigny's engravings; see *The Works of Jonathan Richardson* (London 1792), p. 263.

30 Richardson 1715, p. 115.

31 Public access was fairly restricted until Queen Victoria gave her consent for Hampton Court to be open to the public for five days a week and on Sunday afternoons in November 1838. See Dolman 2017, vol. 29, no. 2, pp. 271–90, esp. p. 273; and Brett Dolman's chapter in this volume.

32 They were actually in line with a school of thought deriving from the art theorist Giovan Pietro Bellori (1613–1696), through the French Fréart de Chambray, André Félibien and Roger de Piles among others, whose works became available in English early in the century and similarly placed Raphael at the apex of history painting. See Meyer 1996, p. 46.

33 Notably this assertion was made in the French translation of Richardson's theoretical works, which advocates a new status for England as a source of aesthetic authority: Richardson Père et Fils, *Traité de la peinture* (Amsterdam 1728), p. 83: 'ce qu'on apèle [*sic*] la *Bible* de Raphael, dont les peintures sont dans le *Vatican*, qui après *Hampton-court*, est le plus riche trésor des Ouvrages de ce divin Peintre'.

34 See Simon 2007, p. 15.

35 The V&A owns three sets of Dorigny's engravings: a bound volume E.656–1996, and two further sets of loose prints 20283 to 20289, and Dyce.2560 to 2566.

36 See for instance Cennino Cennini's *Craftsman's Handbook* (*Libro di Pittura*, 1390s), Leon Battista Alberti, *On Painting* (*De pictura*, 1435), Vasari's introduction to the *Lives of the Most Excellent Painters, Sculptors, and Architects* (1550 and 1568) through to most of the artistic writings of the 15th and the following centuries, fuelled by the foundation of the academies in both Italy and France.

37 For a detailed analysis, see Johns 2009, pp. 501–27. Thornhill had the scenes immediately engraved by a group of various engravers.

38 The painting in Lincoln's Inn, where it still hangs, was subsequently engraved: see example in the Tate (T01805). Hogarth also praised Raphael's art in his *Analysis of Beauty* (1753) but especially after Raphael acknowledged in his work Michelangelo's heroic manner.

39 *The Works of Jonathan Richardson* (London 1792), p. 164ff. Thornhill had planned 'to build an Accademy [*sic*] for Painting' in 1714, a project that never came to life: see Vertue's Note Book 1933, p. 74.

40 Vertue's Note Book 1933, pp. 39 and 43.

41 The title was given in French but the book was an English initiative: *Recueil de XC têtes tirées des sept cartons des Apôtres peint par Raphael Urbin, qui se conservent dans le Palais d'Hampton-Court* (London 1722). A copy is available in the National Art Library: 86.H.22.

42 On the early attempts see Bignamini 1988, pp. 1–148. On the continent, the first Academy to be founded was the Accademia del Disegno in Florence in 1563, followed by the Accademia di San Luca in Rome in 1577. The Académie royale de peinture et de sculpture was founded in Paris in 1648 and the French Academy in Rome in 1666.

43 See Meyer 1996, pp. 39–51. Another set, possibly made for the Duke of Chandos at Canons, was given in 1959 to Columbia University, New York, where they are still on display in the classrooms of the Department of History of Art. Similarly, a set of Mortlake tapestries was given in 1954 to the Cathedral of St John in New York, where they are still in use. I wish to thank Annette Wickham, Curator of Works on Paper at the Royal Academy of Arts, for drawing my attention to this engraving.

44 See Reynolds 1891, esp. pp. 296–341.

45 The Victor Batte-Lay Trust, Colchester: R.95.1; see Graham Reynolds, *The Early Paintings and Drawings of John Constable* (New Haven and London 1996), cat. 95.1–3, p. 5.

46 See also David Blayney Brown, 'Verses, and Note on Perspective in Raphael's Tapestry Cartoon "Paul Preaching at Athens" (Inscriptions by Turner) *c*.1808 by Joseph Mallord William Turner', catalogue entry, March 2007, in *J.M.W. Turner: Sketchbooks, Drawings and Watercolours,*

ed. David Blayney Brown, Tate Research Publication, December 2012, https://www.tate.org.uk/art/research-publications/jmw-turner/joseph-mallord-william-turner-verses-and-note-on-perspective-in-raphaels-tapestry-cartoon-r1130859 (accessed 5 March 2020).

47   On Ruskin's opinion on the Raphael Cartoons see Shearman 1972, pp. 161–2.

48   See Ludwig Grüner, *The Conversion of Saul*, in the V&A (20.399) and *The Stoning of Stephen* in the Royal Collection (RCIN 853075).

49   See the introduction to this volume.

Select Bibliography

Abbreviations
ASF, Archivio di Stato d Firenze
ASMV, Archivio Storico dei Musei Vaticani
ASR, Archivio di Stato di Roma
ASV, Archivio Segreto Vaticano
ABSB, Archivio Bini Smagni Bellarmini
AFSP, Archivio de la Fabbrica di San Pietro
ASMn, Archivio di Stato di Mantova, Archivio Gonzaga
ASMo, Archivio di Stato di Modena, Archivio Estense
BAV, Biblioteca Apostolica Vaticana
BCorr, Biblioteca del Civico Museo Correr, Venezia

Aretino 1999
Pietro Aretino, *Lettere*, ed. Paolo
Procaccioli, III (Rome 1999)

Arisi 1986
Ferdinando Arisi, *Gian Paolo Panini e i fasti
della Roma del '700* (Rome 1986)

Armenini 1587
Giovanni Battista Armenini, *De' veri
precetti della pittura* (Ravenna 1587)

Ballarin 1967
Alessandro Ballarin, 'Jacopo Bassano e
lo studio di Raffaello e dei Salviati', *Arte
Veneta*, XXI (1967), pp. 77–101

Bambach 1999
Carmen Bambach, *Painting and Drawing in the
Italian Renaissance Workshop: Theory and Practice,
1300–1600* (New York and Cambridge 1999)

Bambach-Cappel 1988
Carmen Bambach-Cappel, *The Tradition of
Pouncing Drawings in the Italian Renaissance
Workshop: Innovation and Derivation*,
Ph.D. thesis, Yale University, 1988

Barucca and Ferino-Pagden 2015
Gabriele Barucca and Sylvia Ferino-Pagden,
Raffaello Il Sole delle Arti, exh. cat., Reggia
di Venaria (Cinisello-Balsamo 2015)

Bazzano 2011
Nicoletta Bazzano, 'Ugo Moncada', in
Dizionario Biografico degli Italiani, vol. 75
(Rome 2011)

Becker and Ruland 1863
Dr Ernst Becker and Carl Ruland, '"The Raphael
Collection" of H.R.H. the Prince Consort', *Fine Arts
Quarterly Review*, vol. 1 (May 1863), pp. 27–39

Bickham 1742
George Bickham, *Deliciae Britannicae; Or the Curiosities of Hampton-Court and Windsor-Castle* (London 1742)

Bignamini 1988
Ilaria Bignamini, 'George Vertue, Art Historian and Art Institutions in London, 1689–1768: a Study of Clubs and Academies', *The Volume of the Walpole Society*, vol. 54 (1988), pp. 1–148

Blackmore 1703
Richard Blackmore, *A Hymn to the Light of the World* (London 1703)

Boccardo 2006
Piero Boccardo, 'Le tapezzerie finissime di Fiandra a Genova nel Cinquecento', in *Genova e l'Europa atlantica: opere, artisti, committenti, collezionisti: Inghilterra, Fiandre, Portogallo*, ed. Piero Boccardo and Clario Di Fabio (Cinisello Balsamo-Milan 2006), pp. 111–31

Boydell 1764
John Boydell, 'Description of the Cartoons of Raphael Urbin', *The School of Raphael*, 2nd ed. (London 1764)

Brooks 2015
Julian Brooks with Denise Allen and Xavier F. Salomon, *Andrea del Sarto: The Renaissance Workshop in Action* (Los Angeles 2015)

Browne and Evans 2010
Clare Browne and Mark Evans (eds), *Raphael: Cartoons and Tapestries for the Sistine Chapel* (London 2010)

Bryant 2019
Julius Bryant, *Creating the V&A. Victoria and Albert's Museum (1851–1861)* (London 2019)

Campbell 2002
Thomas Campbell (ed.), *Tapestry in the Renaissance. Art and Magnificence*, exh. cat., Metropolitan Museum of Art, New York (New York 2002)

Campbell 2007
Thomas Campbell, *Henry VIII and the Art of Majesty: Tapestries at the Tudor Court* (New Haven and London 2007)

Caporali 2014
Alessio Caporali, 'Bernardo Bini: un banchiere fiorentino alla corte papale del Rinascimento' in *Progressus*, I, no. 2 (December 2014), pp. 2–27

Caporali 2017
Alessio Caporali, *Bernardo Bini, un banchiere fiorentino alla corte di Leone X: architettura e commissioni artistiche tra Roma e Firenze nel primo Cinquecento*, Ph.D. thesis, University of Florence, 2017; http://hdl.handle.net/2158/1075933 (accessed 20 May 2020)

Castelnuovo 1990
Enrico Castelnuovo (ed.), *Gli arazzi del Cardinale. Bernardo Cles e il ciclo della Passione di Pieter van Aelst* (Trento 1990)

Cicogna 1860
Emanuele Antonio Cicogna, 'Intorno la vita eccelente di M.A. Michiel', *Memorie dell'Istituto Veneto*, IX (1860), p. 405

Clayton 1999
Martin Clayton (ed.), *Raphael and his Circle, Drawings from Windsor Castle*, exh. cat., Queen's Gallery, London (London 1999)

Clayton 2010
Martin Clayton, 'Prince Albert's Raphael Collection' in *Victoria & Albert, Art & Love*, ed. J. Marsden, exh. cat., Queen's Gallery, London (London 2010), pp. 176–7

Cobbett 1806–20
William Cobbett, *The Parliamentary History of England* (London 1806–20)

Cole 1853
Henry Cole, *First Report of the Department of Practical Art* (London 1853)

Cordellier and Py 1992
Dominique Cordellier and Bernadette Py, *Musée du Louvre, Inventaire des dessins italiens. V. Raphaël, son atelier, ses copistes* (Paris 1992)

Dacos 1980
Nicole Dacos, 'Tommaso Vincidor. Un élève de Raphaël aux Pays-Bas' in *Relations artistiques entre les Pays-Bas et l'Italie à la Renaissance* (Brussels 1980), pp. 61–99

Defoe 1724
Daniel Defoe, *A Tour through England and Wales* (London 1724)

Dekker 2013
Rudolf Dekker, *Family, Culture and Society in the Diary of Constantijn Huygens Jr, Secretary to Stadholder-King William of Orange* (Leiden and Boston 2013)

Delmarcel 2020
Guy Delmarcel, 'Pieter van Aelst, fornitore dei papi, e l'industria degli arazzi nelle Fiandre dell'epoca', in *Leone X e Raffaello in Sistina. Gli Arazzi degli Atti degli Apostoli*, ed. Anna Maria De Strobel, 2 vols (Vatican City 2020)

De Strobel 2020
Anna Maria De Strobel (ed.), *Leone X e Raffaello in Sistina. Gli Arazzi degli Atti degli Apostoli*, 2 vols (Vatican City 2020)

De Strobel 2020 (English translation)
Anna Maria De Strobel (ed.), *Leo X and Raphael in the Sistine Chapel. The Tapestries of the Acts of the Apostles*, 2 vols (Vatican City 2020)

De Strobel 2020 – Regesto documentario
Anna Maria De Strobel, Cecilia Mazzetti di Pietralata and M. Checchi, 'Documenti e fonti dei secoli XVI – XIX; Regesto', in *Leone X e Raffaello in Sistina. Gli Arazzi degli Atti degli Apostoli*, ed. Anna Maria De Strobel, 2 vols (Vatican City 2020), pp. 18, 297, 309–10, 325–7, 354

De Strobel and Nesselrath 2010
Anna Maria De Strobel and Arnold Nesselrath, 'The Sistine Chapel tapestries and their Setting' in *Raphael: Cartoons and Tapestries for the Sistine Chapel*, ed. Mark Evans and Clare Browne with Arnold Nesselrath, exh. cat., Victoria and Albert Museum, London (London 2010), pp. 26–9, 31

De Strobel and Nesselrath, 2020
Anna Maria De Strobel and Arnold Nesselrath, 'La commissione e l'allestimento', in *Leone X e Raffaello in Sistina. Gli Arazzi degli Atti degli Apostoli*, ed. Anna Maria De Strobel, 2 vols (Vatican City 2020), pp. 68–78

Diario ordinario 5061
Diario Ordinario, vol. 5061 (Rome 1749)

Diario di Roma 102
Diario di Roma, vol. 102 (Rome 1836)

Dolman 2017
Brett Dolman, 'Curating the Royal Collection at Hampton Court', *Journal of the History of Collections*, vol. 29 (2017), pp. 271–90

Dolman 2018
Brett Dolman, 'From a royal residence to a royal collection', *Journal of the History of Collections*, vol. 30 (2018), pp. 217–33

Fagiolo 1997a
Maurizio Fagiolo, *Corpus delle feste a Roma. La festa barocca*, vol. 1 (Rome 1997)

Fagiolo 1997b
Maurizio Fagiolo, *Corpus delle feste a Roma. Il Settecento e l'Ottocento*, vol. 2 (Rome 1997)

Fagiolo and Madonna 1990
Marcello Fagiolo and Maria Luisa Madonna (eds), *Raffaello e l'europa: atti del 4° Corso internazionale di alta cultura* (Rome 1990)

Faietti and Matteo 2020
Marzia Faietti and Matteo Lafranconi (eds), *Raffaello 1520–1483*, exh. cat., Scuderie del Quirinale, Rome (Rome 2020)

Farington 1978–84
Joseph Farington, *Diary* (New Haven and London 1978–84)

Fermor 1996
Sharon Fermor, *The Raphael Tapestry Cartoons* (London 1996)

Fermor and Derbyshire 1998
Sharon Fermor and Alan Derbyshire, 'The Raphael Tapestry Cartoons Re-Examined', *The Burlington Magazine*, vol. 140, no. 1141 (April 1998), pp. 236–50

Frimmel 1888
Theodor von Frimmel (ed.), *Anonimo Morelliano* (Vienna 1888)

Gastinel Coural 1996
C. Gastinel Coural *La manufacture des Gobelins au XIXe siècle: tapisseries, cartons, maquettes*, exh. cat., Galerie de la Tapisserie, Beauvais (Paris 1996)

Gaye 1839–40
Johann Gaye (ed.) *Carteggio inedito d'artisti dei secoli XIV, XV, XVI*, 3 vols (Florence 1839–40)

Gibson-Wood 2000
Carol Gibson-Wood, *Jonathan Richardson, Art Theorist of the English Enlightment* (New Haven and London 2000)

Gilbert 1987
Creighton Gilbert, 'Are the Ten Tapestries a Complete Series or a Fragment?', in *Studi su Raffaello. Atti del congresso internazionale di Studi (Urbino-Firenze, 6–14 April 1984)*, ed. Micaela Sambucco Hamoud and Maria Letizia Strocchi, vol. I (Urbino 1987), pp. 533–50

Giuliano 2017
Laura Giuliano, *De' pittori, scultori, architetti, minatori et ricamatori napolitani e regnicoli. Le Vite d'artisti di Camilo Tutini (ms del 1664 circa)*, Ph.D. thesis, University of Naples Federico II, 2017; http://www.fecoa.unina.it/11843/1/Giuliano_Laura_29.pdf (accessed 20 May 2020)

Goethe 1983
Johann Wolfgang von Goethe, *Viaggio in Italia*, trans. Emilio Castellani, commentary by Herbert von Einem (Milan 1983)

Golzio 1936
Vincenzo Golzio, *Raffaello nei documenti, nelle testimonianze dei contemporanei e nella letteratura del suo secolo* (Rome 1936)

Heikamp 1969
Detlef Heikamp, 'Die Arazzeria Medicea im 16. Jahrhundert: Neue Studien', *Münchner Jahrbuch der bildenden Kunst*, III. F, 20 (1969), p. 74

Jaffé 1967
Michael Jaffé, 'Rubens and Raphael', *Studies in Renaissance and Baroque Art: Presented to Anthony Blunt on his 60th Birthday* (London and New York 1967), pp. 98–107

Jenkins 1994
Susan Jenkins, 'The Artistic Taste of William III', *The Kings Apartments: Hampton Court Palace* (London 1994), pp. 4–9

Joannides 1983
Paul Joannides, *The Drawings of Raphael: with a complete catalogue* (Oxford 1983)

Johns 2009
Richard Johns, '"An Air of Grandeur & Modesty": James Thornhill's Painting in the Dome of St Paul's Cathedral', *Eighteenth-Century Studies*, vol. 42, no. 4 (Summer 2009), pp. 501–27

Lewis 1937–83
W.S. Lewis (ed.), *The Correspondence of Horace Walpole*, vol. 10 (New Haven and London 1937–83)

Mancinelli 1982
Fabrizio Mancinelli, *Raphael's Tapestries for the Sistine Chapel, in The Vatican Collections. The Papacy and Art*, exh. cat., Metropolitan Museum of Art, New York; Art Institute, Chicago; Fine Arts Museums, San Francisco, (New York 1982)

McParland 2019
Maighread McParland, 'The Acts of the Apostles (copies) at the National Gallery, Dublin. Comments on the Provenance and the Conservation of the Cartoons', *Studia Bruxellae*, no. 13 (2019/1), pp. 325–32

Meyer 1996
Arline Meyer, *Apostles in England: Sir James Thornhill & the Legacy of Raphael's Tapestry Cartoons* (New York 1996)

Montagu 1986
Jennifer Montagu, 'The Ruland/Raphael Collection', *Visual Resources*, vol. III (1986), pp. 167–83

Moroni 1841a
Gaetano Moroni, *Dizionario di erudizione storico-ecclesiastica da San Pietro sino ai nostri giorni*, 103 vols (vol. IX, 1841) (Venice 1840–78)

Moroni 1841b
Gaetano Moroni, *Cappelle pontificie, cardinalizie e prelatizie* (Venice 1841)

Nesselrath 2003
Arnold Nesselrath, 'The Painters of Lorenzo the Magnificent in the Chapel of Pope Sixtus IV in Rome', in *The Fifteenth-Century Frescoes in the Sistine Chapel, Recent Restorations,* Jorge Maria Cardinal Mejìa, Arnold Nesselrath, Pier Nicola Pagliara and Maurizio De Luca, vol. IV (Vatican City 2003), pp. 36–7

Nesselrath 2010
Arnold Nesselrath, 'The Sistine Chapel', in *Raphael: Cartoons and Tapestries for the Sistine Chapel*, ed. Mark Evans and Clare Browne with Arnold Nesselrath, exh. cat., Victoria and Albert Museum, London (London 2010), pp. 21–5

Nesselrath 2019
Arnold Nesselrath, 'The Acts of the Apostles: Raphael's Design Process for Tapestries in the Sistine Chapel', *Studia Bruxellae*, no. 13 (2019/1), pp. 311–23

Oberhuber 1984
Konrad Oberhuber, 'Raffaello e l'incisione' in *Raffaello in Vaticano* (Rome 1984), pp. 333–42

Palme 1957
Per Palme, *Triumph of Peace: A Study of the Whitehall Banqueting House* (London 1957)

Parma 2001
E. Parma (ed.), *Perino del Vaga tra Raffaello and Michelangelo*, exh. cat., Palazzo Te, Mantua (Milan 2001)

Pastor 1905
Antonio de Beatis, *Die Reise des Kardinals Luigi d'Aragona durch Deutschland, die Niederlande, Frankreich und Oberitalien*, 1517–18, ed. Ludwig von Pastor (Freiburg im Breisgau, Munich 1905)

Pastor 1956
Ludwig von Pastor, *Storia dei papi dalla fine del Medio Evo*, ed. Angelo Mercati (rev. Italian ed., Rome 1944–63), 20 vols; vol. IV, *Storia dei papi nel periodo del rinascimento e dello scisma luterano dall'elezione di Leone X alla morte di Clemente VII (1513–1534)*, t. 2, *Adriano VI e Clemente VII* (Rome 1956)

Pastor 1960
L. von Pastor, *Storia dei papi dalla fine del medio evo*, ed. Angelo Mercati (rev. Italian ed.), 20 vols (Rome 1944–63); vol. IV, *Storia dei papi nel periodo del rinascimento e dello scisma luterano dall'elezione di Leone X alla morte di Clemente VII (1513–1534)*, t. 1, *Leone X* (Rome 1960)

Perronet 1995–8
Benjamin Perronet (ed.), *Dessins italiens du musée Condé à Chantilly. v. 2. Raphaël et son cercle* (Paris 1995–8)

Physick 1975
John Physick, *Photography and the South Kensington Museum* (London 1975)

Physick 1982
John Physick, *The Victoria and Albert Museum: The History of its Building* (London 1982)

Pietrangeli 1985
Carlo Pietrangeli, *I Musei Vaticani: cinque secoli di storia* (Rome 1985)

Plesters 1990
Joyce Plesters, 'Raphael's Cartoons for the Vatican Tapestries: A Brief report on the Materials, Technique and Condition', in *The Princeton Raphael Symposium*, ed. John Shearman and Marcia B. Hall (Princeton, NJ 1990), pp. 111–24

Pope 1960–3
Willard Bissell Pope (ed.), *The Diary of Benjamin Haydon*, vol. 4 (Cambridge 1960–3)

Reynolds 1891
Sir Joshua Reynolds, *Discourses*, ed. Edward Gilpin Johnson (Chicago 1891)

Richardson 1715
Jonathan Richardson, *Essay on the Theory of Painting* (London 1715, repr. 1725)

Roberts 1995
Helene E. Roberts (ed.), *Art History through the Camera's Lens* (Amsterdam 1995)

Rohlmann 2003
Michael Rohlmann, 'Raffaels Vatikanisches "Bilderzeremoniell" Grenzüberschreitungen in der Sixtinischen Kapelle und den Stanzen', in *Functions and decorations: Art and Ritual at the Vatican Palace in the Middle Ages and the Renaissance*, ed. Tristan Weddigen, Sible De Blaauw and Bram Kempers ('Capellae Apostolicae Sixtinaeque Collectanea Acta Monumenta', V) (Vatican City 2003), pp. 95–108

Rosenberg 1995
Martin Rosenberg, *Raphael and France, the Artist as Paradigm and Symbol* (London 1995)

Ruland 1866
Carl Ruland, 'Proposed Exhibition of Raphael's Works' in *Notes on the Cartoons of Raphael now in the South Kensington Museum and on Raphael's other works* (London 1866), pp. 11–12

Ruland 1876
Carl Ruland, *The Works of Raphael Santi da Urbino as represented in the Raphael Collection in the Royal Library at Windsor Castle, Formed by H.R.H. The Prince Consort, 1853–1861 and completed by Her Majesty Queen Victoria* (London 1876)

Russell 1987
Francis Russell, 'King George III's picture hang at Buckingham House', *The Burlington Magazine*, vol. 129, no. 1013 (August 1987), pp. 524–31

Saint-Aubin 1770
Charles-Germain de Saint-Aubin, *L'art du brodeur* (Paris 1770)

Sanudo, *Diarii*
Marin Sanudo, *I diarii (MCCCXCVI – MDXXXIII)*, Unveränderter Nachdruck der Aufl. (Venice 1879–1903, Bologna 1959–70)

Shearman 1972
John Shearman, *Raphael's Cartoons in the Collection of Her Majesty the Queen, and the Tapestries for the Sistine Chapel* (London 1972)

Shearman 2003
John Shearman, *Raphael in Early Modern Sources (1483–1602)*, 2 vols (New Haven and London 2003)

Simon 2007
Robin Simon, *Hogarth, France and British Art: the rise of the arts in eighteenth-century Britain* (London 2007)

Smith 1993
Hillie Smith, 'The Tapestry Collection of Pope Julius II (1503–13): Notes by Marcantonio Michiel in 1519', *Bulletin du CIETA*, no. 71 (1993), pp. 48–60

Steele 1711
Richard Steele, *The Spectator*, no. 226 (19 November 1711)

Steinmann 1897
Ernst Steinmann, *Cancellata und Cantoria in der Sixtinischen Kapelle* (Berlin 1897) in *Jahrbuch der Preußischen Kunstsammlungen*, XVIII (1897)

Thompson 1878
Edward Maunde Thompson (ed.), *Correspondence of the Family of Hatton*, vol. 2 (London 1878)

Thomson 1914
William George Thomson, *Tapestry Weaving in England* (London 1914)

Thurley 2003
Simon Thurley, *Hampton Court Palace: A Social and Architectural History* (New Haven and London 2003)

Turriziani 2020
Simona Turriziani, 'Gli arazzi di Raffaello sulle terrazze della Basilica di San Pietro per la visita di Ferdinando IV di Borbone nel 1791', in *La Basilica di San Pietro, Notiziario mensile a cura della Fabbrica di San Pietro*, Anno XXXII (May 2020), no. 5, pp. 2–3.

Vasari 1568
Giorgio Vasari, *Le vite de' più eccellenti pittori, scultori, e architettori* (Florence 1568)

Vasari 1963
Giorgio Vasari, *The Lives of the Painters, Sculptors and Architects*, trans. A.B. Hinds (London 1963)

Vasari 1966–87
Giorgio Vasari, *Le vite de' più eccellenti pittori scultori e architettori: nelle redazioni del 1550 e 1568*, ed. Rosanna Bettarini and Paola Barocchi (Florence 1966–87)

Vasari 1981
Giorgio Vasari, *Le vite de' più eccellenti pittori, scultori ed architettori scritte da Giorgio Vasari, pittore aretino con nuove annotazioni e commenti di Gaetano Milanesi*, vol. I (Florence 1906, repr. 1981)

Vertue 1929–30
The Notebooks of George Vertue relating to Artists and Collections in England, Walpole Society, vol. 1 (Oxford 1929–30)

Walpole 1928
Horace Walpole's Journal of Visits to Country Seats, Walpole Society, vol. 16 (Oxford 1928)

Weddigen 1998/9
Tristan Weddigen, *Tappiseriekunst unter Leo X. Raffaels Apostelgeschicte für die Sixtinische Kapelle in Hoch Renaissance im Vatikan 1503–1534. Kunst und Kultur im Rom der Päpste*, exh. cat., Bundeskunsthalle, Bonn (Ostfildern-Ruit 1998)

Weddingen 2006
Tristan Weddigen, *Raffaels Papageienzimmer: Ritual, Raumfunktion und Dekoration im Vatikanpalast der Renaissance* (Berlin 2006)

White and Shearman 1958
John White and John Shearman, 'Raphael's Tapestries and Their Cartoons', *Art Bulletin*, 40 (1958), pp. 193–221

Wyld 2018
Helen Wyld, 'Charles I and Raphael's Acts of the Apostles', in *Charles I. King and Collector*, ed. Desmond Shawe-Taylor and Per Rumberg, exh. cat., Royal Academy, London (London 2018), pp. 190–205

Acknowledgements

This book accompanies the essential renovation project of the Raphael Court in 2020, which has been made possible through close collaboration with the Vatican Museums and Royal Collection Trust, as well as the assistance of numerous colleagues at the V&A and other institutions. The project was supported by Lydia & Manfred Gorvy, Julia and Hans Rausing, American Express, the Royal Commission for the Exhibition of 1851, Sir Michael and Lady Hintze, the Robert H. Smith Family Foundation, the American Friends of the V&A, and many other generous donors.

We would like to thank all the members of the Raphael Project Team at the V&A; Coralie Hepburn, Sophie Sheldrake, Kirstin Beattie, Denny Hemming, Emma Woodiwiss and Andrew Tullis for their work on this book; the co-authors Alessandra Rodolfo and Brett Dolman; Tristram Hunt and Antonia Boström for their trust. For many rich and fruitful exchanges, we would also like to thank: Hélène Bartelloni-Cascio, Guido Beltramini, Pascal Bertrand, Giulio Bora, Clare Browne, Julius Bryant, Thomas Campbell, Hugo Chapman, Martin Clayton, Katherine Coombs, Dominique Cordellier, Clara de la Peña McTigue, Guy Delmarcel, Marco Delogu, Alan Derbyshire, Francesco Paolo Di Teodoro, Valentine Dubard, David Ekserdjian, Caroline Elam, Sylvia Ferino-Padgen, Hélène Gasnault, Ana Gonzales Mozo, Tom Henry, David Jaffé, Paul Joannides, Lorraine Karafel, Emily Knight, Tim Knox, Stefan Koja, Matteo Lafranconi, Adam Lowe and his wonderful team at Factum Foundation, Morgane Lucquet-Laforgue, Michelle O'Malley, Maurizio Michelozzi, Arnold Nesselrath, Joanna Norman, Richard Palmer, Nicholas Penny, Ella Ravilious, Jana Riedel, Phil Sanderson, Gill Saunders, Bill Sherman, Ben Thomas, Catherine Whistler, Tom Windross and Matthias Wivel.

At the Vatican Museums, we would like to thank Barbara Jatta, Monsignor Paolo Nicolini, Roberto Romano, Guido Cornini, Michela Gianfranceschi, Rosanna Di Pinto, Filippo Petrignani and Simona Turriziani. We would also like to thank Claudio A. M. Salsi, Alessia Alberti and Maria Rita D'Amato at Castello Sforzesco in Milan; Alessio Caporali and Luisa Capodieci at Université Paris 1 Panthéon-Sorbonne, and many more.

The authors are particularly indebted to the seminal study on Raphael's Cartoons by John Shearman, *Raphael's Cartoons in the Collection of Her Majesty the Queen and the Tapestries for the Sistine Chapel* (London 1972); as well as on their history in England by Arline Meyer, *Apostles in England* (New York 1996).

Picture Credits

Index

Page numbers in *italic* refer to the illustrations

Act of Toleration (1689) — 65
Acts of the Apostles — 29, 47, *49*, 51, 52
Aelst, Pieter van — 38, 47
Albert, Prince Consort — 7, 11–12, 14–15, 73
Alcántara, St Pedro de — 56
Andrea del Sarto — 79
Andrew, St — 19
Angerstein, John — 72
Anne, Queen of England — 66, 67
Aragona, Cardinal Luigi d' — 47
Arundel Society — 93
Audran, Gérard — *84*, 85–6

Bache, William — 63
Banqueting House, Whitehall — 63, 81, 83
Barnabas, St — 24
Basilica of St Peter, Rome — 27, 39, 56–9
Basilica of San Lorenzo, Florence — 39
Beatis, Antonio de — 47, 48
Becker, Ernst — 14
Beltrami, Luca — 60, 61, *61*
Benedict XIV, Pope — 56, *57*
Benintendi, Antonio de' — *29*
Bibbiena, Cardinal — 39, 77
Bini, Bernardo — 47, 54
Bini, Giovanni — 54
Bini, Piero — 54
Blackmore, Richard — 65
borders — 31, 81, 83–4
Botticelli, Sandro — 27
Boughton House, Northamptonshire — 83
Bourbon, Charles de — 54
Boydell, John — 68
Bramante, Donato — 39
Brancacci Chapel, Florence — 40
British Institution — 71
Brussels — 38, 42, 47, 81, 82
Buccleuch, Duke of — 17, 83
Buckingham House/Palace, London — 68–70, *69*, 71
Burton, J. Davis — *16*

Camuccini, Vincenzo — 60
Caporali, Alessio — 47
Caroline, Queen — 67
cartoons (*cartone*) — 31–5, 41–2
Castiglione, Baldassare — 54
ceramics — 79, *79*
Chambers, William — 68
Charles I, King — 81–2, 83–4, 85, 87
Charles II, King — 70

Charles V, Emperor — 81
Charlotte, Queen — 68
Chiericati, Francesco — 48
Chigi, Agostino — 54
Christ — 19–20, 27, 34, 41, 48, 50, 53, 57, 59
Christ's Charge to Peter — 15, 20, *20*, 29, 34, 36, *36*, 42, *43*, 70, 71, 73, 92
Cleyn, Francis — 82–3, *82*
Coecke van Aeslt, Pieter — 40
Cole, Henry — 12, 13, 15
Colonna family — 54, 56
Consalvi, Cardinal — 59
Constable, John — 92
The Conversion of the Proconsul — 23, *23*, 29–31, 33, *33*, 54, 55, 59, 70, 71, 77, 79, *79*
The Conversion of Saul — 29, 31, 41, 54, 55, 82
Cooke, Henry — 63
Corpus Christi, Feast of — 57–8, 60
counterproof — 36–7
Courteys, Martial — *79*
Crane, Sir Francis — 82
Cromwell, Oliver — 84–5

Dalton, Richard — 68, 70
Davis, John Scarlett — *67*
De Strobel, Anna Maria — 50–2
The Death of Ananias — 22, *22*, 29, 44, 70, 71, 77, *79*, 82, *84*, 85–6
Department of Science and Art — 14
Diario di Roma — 60
Dorigny, Sir Nicolas — 66, 87–8, *88*, 90, 92

Eastlake, Sir Charles — 15
Edward VII, King — 75
Elymas — 23
Este, Antonio d' — 60
Este, Isabella d' — 48
Ewart, William — 71

Fabbrica di San Pietro — 59
Farington, Joseph — 70, 71
Ferdinand IV, King of Naples — 59
Florence — 40, 79, 82
Floreria — 54, 56, 59
Francis I, King of France — 55, 56, 81
Fregoso, Cesare — 55

Galilee, Sea of — 19
Genoa — 40, 42, 82
George, Prince Regent — 71
George I, King — 88

George III, King 68, 70, 71
Ghirlandaio, Domenico 27
Gibbons, Grinling 64
Giovanni da Udine 37–8, 39
Giulio Romano 38, 39, 40
Gobelins Manufactory, Paris 59
Goethe, Johann Wolfgang von 59
Gonzaga, Cardinal Ercole 81
Gonzaga, Federico, Duke of Mantua 54
Gospel of John 20
Gospel of Matthew 20
Grassis, Paris de 45, 48, 50
Gregory XVI, Pope 60
Gribelin, Simon II 66, *66*, 86–7, *86*
Grimani, Cardinal 41
Guillaumot, Charles-Axel 59

Hadrian VI, Pope 54
Hampton Court Palace 11, 13–15, *13*, 63–8, *64*, *69*,
 70–5, *74*, 85, 87
Hatton, Charles 63
Hatton, Christopher, Viscount Hatton 63
Haydon, Benjamin 72
The Healing of the Lame Man 21, *21*, 29, 57
Henry VIII, King *80*, 81, 82
Hogarth, William 88
Holloway, Thomas 71
Hunt, William Holman 93
Huygens, Constantijn 63

Innocent XIII, Pope 56

James, St 19
James II, King 65
Jervas, Charles 63, 85–6
John, St 19, 21
Jones, Inigo 83
Julius II, Pope 27, 28, 54
Jupiter 24

Kinnersley, Philip 63
Kneller, Sir Godfrey 63

Landsknechte mercenaries 54
Lawrence, Sir Thomas 71, *91*
LeBlon, James-Christopher 66
Leo X, Pope 7, 11, 25, *25*, 27, 28, *29*, 31, 39, 41–2, 47,
 48, 52, 53–4, 65, 81
Leonardo da Vinci 11, 58
Limoges 79, *79*
Lippi, Filippino 40

Logge 39, 60
Louis XIV, King of France 65, 85
Luti, Margherita 78

Mantegna, Andrea 84–5
Mantua 40, 81
Marco (Dente) da Ravenna 77
Maria Carolina of Austria 59
Mary II, Queen 63–4
Masaccio, Tommaso Giovanni di 40
Mazzone, Monsignor 60
Medici, Ferdinando I de' 56
Medici, Ferdinando II de' 82
Medici, Cardinal Francesco Armellini de' 53–4
Medici, Lorenzo de' (the Magnificent) 27
Mercury 24
Michelangelo 11, 28, 42, 52, 55, 92
Michiel, Marcantorio 45, 48, 55
Millais, John Everett 93
The Miraculous Draught of Fishes 17, 19, *19*, 29, 32,
 34–5, *34–5*, 38, 50, 52, 77
Moncada, Don Ugo de 55–6
Montmorency, Anne de 55
Mortlake 15, 17, 82–3, *82–3*, 85
Moses 27, 41, 50, 53
Museum of Manufactures 12

Napoleon I, Emperor 59
Nash, John 71
National Gallery, London 15, 71–2, *73*
Netherlands 29, 40, 42
New Testament 50, 65–6
Nicholas III, Pope 27
Norris, John 63
Nost, John 64

Old Testament 50
Orley, Bernard van 40
Ottaviano, Giovanni 57, *58*

Palazzo Venier, Venice 55
Panini, Francesco 57, *58*
Panini, Giovanni Paolo 56–7, *57*
Patanazzi workshop 79
Paul, St 23, 24, 25, *25*, 29, 50, 65
Paul III, Pope 55
Paul in Prison 31, 50, 59, 82
Paul Preaching at Athens 25, *25*, 31, 54, 55, 70, 77,
 78, *79*, 92, *92*
Pauline cycle 29–31, 50
Pazzi, St Maddalena dei 56

Pellipario, Nicola 79
Pembroke, Earl of 83
Penni, Giovanni Francesco 37, 38, 39
The Pentecost (tapestry) 57
Pericoli, Nicola 60
Perino del Vaga 39, 40
Perugino, Pietro 27, 28
Peter, St 19, 20, *20*, 22, 23, 27, 29, 50, 65
Petrine cycle 29, 31, 50
Philip II, King of Spain 81
photography 13–14
Pius VI, Pope 56, 59, 60
Pius VII, Pope 59, 60
Pius XI, Pope 60
Poussin, Nicolas 79
Pre-Raphaelite Brotherhood 93
Protestants 65–6

Raimondi, Marcantonio 77, *78*
Ralph, Benjamin 90
Raphael Collection 11, 12–17, *14*
Raphael Hall, Vatican 60–1, *61*
Redgrave, Richard 13, 15, 73, 75
Reynolds, Sir Joshua 91, 92
Richardson, Jonathan 68, 87, 88, 89
Rossetti, Dante Gabriel 93
Royal Academy 71, 91–2, 93
Royal Collection 13, 33, 75
Royal Library, Windsor Castle 14, *14*
Royal Mausoleum, Frogmore 12
Rubens, Peter Paul 82, 83
Ruland, Carl 14, 15–16
Ruskin, John 93

Sack of Rome (1527) 45, 54, 55–6
The Sacrifice at Lystra 24, *24*, 31, 36, *36*, 70, *83*, *84*, 85–6
St Paul's Cathedral, London 88
San Michele Manufactory, Rome 60
Sanudo, Marin 55
Scala Regia 57–8
School of Design 12
screen (*transenna*) 50, 53
Sebastiano del Piombo 72
Seguier, William 72
Select Committee on Art 71, 72
Sergius Paulus 23
Shearman, John 48–50, 55, 85
Signorelli, Luca 27
Sistine Chapel 7, 11, 14, 17, 27–8, *30*, 40–1, 42, 48–53, *49*, *51*, *53*, 54–5, 56, 93

Sixtus IV, Pope 27–8
sketches (*schizzo*) 32, 33, 35
Slaughter, Stephen 68
Solomon's Temple, Jerusalem 21
South Kensington Museum 11, 12–17, 73, 75
Steele, Richard 66
The Stoning of Stephen 29, 31, 50–1, 52, 82
Stuart dynasty 65
Stufetta 39, 77

Talman, William 64
Thompson, Charles Thurston *12–13*, 14, *73*
Thornhill, Sir James 66, 88–91, *89*
Turner, Joseph Mallord William 92, *92*
Tutini, Camillo 55, 56

Ugo da Carpi 77
Uwins, Thomas 72–3

Vasari, Giorgio 28, 31, 32, 33, 35, 37–40, 42, 45, 77, 79
Vatican Museums 60–1
Vatican Palace 11, 27–8, 39, *58*, 87
Vatican Stanze 28, 39, 40, 87
Veneziano, Agostino 77
Venice 55
Verrio, Antonio 70
Vertue, George 86, 87
Victoria, Crown Princess of Prussia 14–15
Victoria, Queen 7, 11, 12, 14–15, 73
Villa Madama, Rome 39
Volkman, Johann Jacob 70

Walpole, Horace 68, 70
Walton, Parry 63
Welser, Johann 54
West, Benjamin 70, 71, 72, 91, *91*
Whitehall Palace, London 81
Wilkes, John 68
Wilkins, William 72
William III, King 11, 63–5, 70, 75, 85
Windsor Castle 12, 14, *14*, 70
Wingfield, James Digman *64*
Wren, Sir Christopher 85